CHURCHES IN EXILE

Dedication

This book has evolved from an inter-church Women and Peace-building course, which was taught as part of the Irish School of Ecumenics Education for Reconciliation programme. The course was offered in four locations: Armagh, Belfast, Dungannon and Monaghan, and approximately ninety women participated. Their responses to the course material informed my thinking and supplemented the ongoing library research necessary for the writing of each chapter.

It is for this reason that I dedicate this book to the women who took part in the adult education course. I hope that this resource will prove helpful to other study groups or individuals interested in engaging the theme of churches in exile.

Cathy Higgins

Churches in Exile

Alternative Models of Church for
Ireland in the 21st Century

the columba press

First edition, 2013, published by
the columba press
55A Spruce Avenue, Stillorgan Industrial Park,
Blackrock, Co. Dublin

Origination by The Columba Press
Printed by SPRINT-print, Dublin

ISBN 978 1 85607 838 2

Contents

Introduction

All Change

Change is one of life's constants and is inevitable and un-avoidable. The survival of any life species, or any social, cultural, economic or religious system is dependent on its ability to adapt and endure.

We are living at a time of significant religio-political change in the western world. Churches are no longer at the centre of power in the public square and have been pushed, or exiled, to the margins of civic society. The Christendom model of belief is gradually breaking down and being replaced by faith as openness to the mystery of God and to God's future. There is a trend away from hierarchical, patriarchal and institutional religion. Those who identify as post-Christendom people are more interested in ethical guidelines and spiritual disciplines than in doctrines, dogmas or systems of belief. Post-Christendom faith is increasingly being equated with living ethically in God's world.

The biblical experience of exile provides a rich metaphor for those grappling with the changing social context and the challenges to faith presented by this new reality. For the Hebrew people, the exile was an experience of dislocation and redefinition, death and rebirth, endings and fresh beginnings. In exile, they began to reappraise their perception of God and re-describe their faith world. The renewal that followed was so profound and all-embracing it inspired the collection and writing of much of the Hebrew Scriptures.

The Christian Church in Ireland is at a *kairos* moment in its history, which if embraced has the potential to lead eventually to the reconstruction and revisioning of our God-images, our understanding of community and our ways of being church.

Communities of faith shaped by context

Communities of faith are communities of theological reflection. They are constantly shaping and reshaping their God-images.

These faith communities are spiritual entities but that is not the whole story, though churches frequently wish that it was and often present themselves and their histories as spiritual. In reality, they are also sociological entities rooted in history, politics and economics, and are never communities above, or outside, of these dynamics. They are the products of history and all that that means, are shaped by the dynamics of history around them and in turn make their own contribution to shaping history and politics. God-talk, therefore, is never purely spiritual, above or outside of history. Faith communities may talk about the revelation of God but even God does not bypass historical and political experience. The Word always becomes flesh with all the limitations and complexities of being flesh. Theology, therefore, is always in context. We can only talk about the 'Word that became flesh' within all the dynamics and contingencies of flesh.

All theology is earthed, contextual and incarnational. The spirit is only found in the material, the historical and the secular. This has implications for how we do theology and be church. The church is, consequently, a human–spiritual institution with the challenge to engage sacred secularity and reflect in word and action the sacredness of the secular. This is why this moment in history is the moment to speak of God and to be church in context. We cannot do God-talk, or be people of faith in another world, even though we draw on the foundational roots of our faith from a world and a context of another time. Biblical texts also have historical contexts but these texts have a surplus of meaning. The task of a faith community is to engage its primary texts in their sociopolitical context through interaction with the contemporary sociopolitical context. This allows the radical and subversive nature of the texts to stand both in their original world and our contemporary world. It can also ensure that the church is not a community of the status quo, in collaboration with the world, in love with political power, but a counter-cultural movement, which in humility dares to embody otherness in the secular and public here and now. Churches are therefore called to be communities of radical and subversive theological reflection.

This approach to theology in context, and being church in context, is what underpins this book. It is essentially a book of theological reflection, which takes seriously the current historical context, in which theological reflection and action occur. Negative and destructive theologies have emerged from our Irish historical experience of violence and sectarianism and our being an integral part of Christendom, with its corrupting dynamic of faith aligned with political power. If theology is to be transformative in the present and create transforming and transformative communities then critical engagement with history and context is required; as is critical engagement with faith's foundational texts. Key to this book is critical engagement with the paradigm of exile, drawn from Ancient Israel's experience, and suggestive of the churches' current experience in Ireland. At the heart of that exilic experience there emerged creativity and hope. Out of exile came a new identity, a new sense of purpose and a new vision of God. If this is a *kairos* moment in our history then the creative potential of exile is open to us also.

Mapping the theological scene

The purpose of the book is to suggest alternative models of church and faith that might provide inspiration and hope for the exilic journey ahead.

Chapter 1, *Churches: Shaped By and Shaping Context*, takes as a starting point the various crises facing the church-going community in Ireland. It also critiques violence, sectarianism and exclusive truth claims from the standpoint of history and theology, demonstrating how these stark realities have been shaped by, and shape, church.

Chapter 2, *Living with the End of Christendom*, attempts to analyse the changing situation for Irish churches. It looks briefly at the development of the Christendom model and its breakdown in the Eurocentric world. Also the implications of this for churches no longer at the centre of arrangements of power, or with the privilege and status they once had.

As already suggested, the exile profoundly shaped Ancient Israel's understanding of its identity and purpose. It pushed the Hebrews to reimagine what it meant to live as a minority community covenanted to Yahweh in the shadow of empire. Chapter 3, *The Hebrew Scriptures: Fashioned by Exile*, critically engages the exilic experience as a key paradigm for contemporary Irish faith communities.

Chapter 4, *Models of Church in the Christian Testament*, explores the reality that in the Christian Testament there is no one normative model of church. The diversity of models, which can provide inspiration for contemporary Irish churches, include: a religio-political model of church in Thessalonica; an equality model of church in Galatia; a just economic model of church in Corinth; a kenotic model of power in the Philippian church and church as sign of the kingdom of God in Matthew.

Chapter 5, *Looking Forward to our Celtic Roots*, explores monastic models of ministry and the role women played in the Celtic Church. Particular attention is paid to how some of the Celtic insights on community, spirituality, ecology and restorative justice speak to contemporary ethical challenges.

Chapter 6, *Learning from the Peace Churches*, explores the origins and alternative counter-cultural peace witness of the Anabaptist–Mennonites and Society of Friends in Ireland and further afield. The God of redemptive violence is the antithesis of the Peace Churches' affirmation of a God of life and wisdom, who inspires the move from violence to just-relations and peace. The active, non-violent, religio-political perspective shared by the Peace Churches provides an alternative model to Irish churches still hidebound by theologies that can be used to justify violence, sexism and sectarianism.

Chapter 7, *Recovering a Discipleship of Equals for the Church*, considers twenty-first-century women's experience of church, in light of Jesus' and Paul's critique of patriarchy and endorsement of a discipleship of equals. The recovery of this equality model for Irish churches is the primary focus.

The final chapter, *New Wine, New Wineskins: What is emerging in the 21st century?*, explores new forms of church emerging. It takes account of the influence of postmodernity and post-evangelicalism on the emerging movement. Core practices and values of the emerging models of church are outlined. And, creative responses by emerging churches to issues of power, leadership, equality, inclusively and interfaith ethics are also considered.

The research, writing and publication of this book, was made possible by the grant given to the Irish School of Ecumenics by the International Fund for Ireland. I am grateful for this opportunity to thank them for their financial support. I also wish to thank the Irish School of Ecumenics Trustees and Steering Committee, who have supported the work of the Education for Reconciliation programme since its inception.

Finally, particular thanks to my colleague, Johnston McMaster, for his encouragement, listening ear, and insightful comments and suggestions.

CHAPTER ONE

Churches: Shaped By and Shaping Context

The main focus of this book is the future of church in Ireland. It is my conviction that the starting point for any discussion has to be with present experience, which means understanding sociopolitical, historical, theological and cultural contexts that have impacted current expressions of church. My contention is that the way churches have evolved in Ireland needs to be understood before visioning new ways of being church.

Abuses of power, lack of leadership, cover-up, mismanagement, criminality, and sinfulness, are words used by the media in Northern Ireland with some frequency in the last few years to describe the crises experienced within economic, political and religious institutions, locally and globally. People in Ireland are not without experience of dealing with crises. The thirty plus years of the Troubles showed us that while all are to some extent negatively impacted by the environment of violence and sectarianism, not all suffer to the same extent. Those who lost their lives and survivors who lost limbs, families, and loved ones, have borne the brunt of our war with each other.

The present economic downturn resulting from financial mismanagement has left some without jobs, homes, and savings. In 2010 the Evangelical Fundamentalist constituency was shaken by revelations from within the Democratic Unionist Party (DUP). The Ferns, Ryan, Murphy and Cloyne Reports exposed abuses within Catholic institutions, and the suffering experienced by victims and survivors of abuse, exacerbated by efforts to cover these up.

There are a number of ways to deal with a crisis. The economic focus has been on bailing out the banks, increasing national debt, cutting public spending, in an effort to move out of recession. Yet we still hear of banking corporations, some owned in part by tax payers, paying massive bonuses to employees. What lessons have been learnt? Is the question of ethical responsibility even considered?

In Northern Ireland the relationship between unionism and evangelicalism is one of shifting sand. For some members of the DUP politics are based on a theocratic model of governance. God rules society and God's laws are meant to be the basis of society. However, political dynamics and realism of recent times show that theocracy does not work. In fact, theocracy in history has never worked, as Calvin's failed experiment in Geneva also showed. This realisation has confused many in the evangelical fundamentalist constituency and is a seismic shock to this whole theological system. It also shatters the model of faith and politics and opens up the whole question, what is the relationship between faith and politics in a pluralistic, participative democracy?

The systemic failure of Catholic institutions in Ireland to protect the vulnerable in their care, and culpability in covering up abuse scandals, underlines the need for a root and branch transformation of the church, and the social and political institutions that colluded with it. The First Minister Peter Robinson's announcement in 2011 that Northern Ireland is to have its own major inquiry into clerical abuse of children in institutions run by the Catholic Church and the state is an important development. The Northern Irish victims, who have already found voice, deserve at least this. The ramifications of the various reports have enormous implications for the Catholic Church, all the way from local level to the system in the Vatican itself. We are dealing here with root shock among Catholic people and to the Catholic theological system. Catholicism, like evangelical fundamentalism, has suffered a detrimental upset to its moral authority in Ireland. Faith and systems need to be radically revisioned and this can only be done if there is a reconnecting with the deepest roots of faith and faith resources in the Judeo-Christian foundational documents.

History has taught us that if we do not learn from the mistakes of the past we are likely to repeat them. We have the opportunity to take stock of where we are economically, politically and religiously and consider what changes need to be exercised to protect and empower the most vulnerable in our society and world. This will mean looking at the way power, leadership and accountability are managed within the systems and institutions which order society, including church. But to meet this challenge fully we also need to engage in an honest critique of other key factors, namely violence, sectarianism and exclusive truth claims, which have negatively impacted religious, sociopolitical and economic relations and institutions like the churches in Ireland.

Violence

The culture of violence in Ireland is not only pervasive but also historical. Tracing the historical roots of violence is difficult because of the contested nature of much of our history. Did patterns of violence begin in the twelfth century, the seventeenth century, the nineteenth century, or the early twentieth century? It is possible to trace a thread through all of these centuries. But the seventeenth century is the one that has had the greatest impact on the patterns of violent relationships in the north-east of Ireland. William Maguire, in his recent book on the history of Belfast, has no difficulty tracing episodes of sectarian violence from Plantation to the twenty-first century.[1] What form did sectarian violence take in Ireland; and what legacy has it bequeathed us?

In 1609 James I produced his *Articles of Plantation*. Plantation was a carefully thought out government strategy to subdue a very troublesome region of Ireland, namely Ulster, which had been the last bastion of Gaelic independence. The purpose of the Articles was also to replace the false religion of Catholicism with the true faith of Protestantism. The Planters, who arrived in the north-east of Ireland, included English and Welsh, but were largely Scottish. The most significant thing about the Scots was their Presbyterianism, which introduced the Reformed model of the Reformation to Ireland. Patterns of social, religious and political conflict were immediately created and violence between native Gael and Planter became inevitable. The Planters set about tilling the land and building towns. Farmhouses, which were defensive bawns, were erected. It was said that people farmed the land with the spade in one hand and a sword in the other. An insecure and

---

1. William Maguire, *Belfast: A History* (Lancaster: Carnegie Publishing Ltd, 2009).

fearful settler community had its worst nightmares realised when a Catholic rising occurred in 1641 with the drowning of many Protestants in the river Bann. A Scottish Covenantal army landed on Irish shores to crush the rebellion, with some victories and some defeats. In 1649 Cromwell arrived intent on vengeance, massacring thousands at Drogheda and Wexford. His policy of displacement resulted in many native Irish being relocated to the west of Ireland – 'to hell or to Connacht'.

Between 1689 and 1691 a series of battles were fought on Irish soil between the armies of William of Orange and James II. They began with the Siege of Derry and ended with the Siege and Treaty of Limerick. Though these battles have been interpreted by Protestants in the north-east of Ireland as a Protestant military victory over Catholics, the Williamite wars were more complex. They were a consequence of European power politics played out on Irish soil. The seventeenth century was a century of religious wars in Ireland, as it had been elsewhere in Europe. But in Ireland it left patterns and a legacy of sectarian violence which has not gone away.

By 1704 Queen Anne, William's successor, had strengthened the Penal Laws which, supported by the established Church of Ireland, were oppressive of Catholics and Presbyterians. Not surprisingly, radical Presbyterians gave birth to the United Irishmen, who were the founders of modern day Irish Republicanism and were in the vanguard of the 1798 Rising. There were also Presbyterians in the yeomanry and on the government side in a rising which claimed at least fifty thousand lives in a matter of months. The objectives of the United Irishmen to unite Protestant, Catholic and Dissenter, reform the Irish parliament and introduce greater equality of relationships and justice in Ireland, were defeated by sectarian violence.

The nineteenth century brought in Catholic Emancipation in 1829, witnessed a number of unsuccessful and even botched risings and saw an unsuccessful campaign for the repeal of the Act of Union in 1800. The rest of the nineteenth century was dominated by the Land War and in the last two decades by the failure of two Home Rule bills for Ireland. The Home Rule bills of 1886 and 1893 were characterised by violence and killing and a growing threat of even greater violence.

The third Home Rule Bill of 1912 saw the formation of the illegal Ulster Volunteer Force and the setting up of a treasonous provisional government for the north-east of Ireland if the British imposed Home Rule. This was followed by gun running that resulted in the militarisation of Irish politics in the twentieth century, and which was then emulated by the setting up of the Irish Volunteers with guns obtained from similar German sources. The gun was well and truly established in Irish politics.

The Ulster Covenant of 1912 pledged to 'use any means necessary to defeat this conspiracy'. Irish Republicans looked on at apparent Unionist success and thought they could have the same. In 1916 the Easter Rising occurred in Dublin and was easily defeated; but the execution of fifteen of its leaders by the British authorities turned the rising into a defining moment in Irish history. The Proclamation of 1916 was rooted in violence and, like the Covenant, invoked a violent god.

The pervasive culture of violence was well and truly established and it was the obsession with violence which, more than anything else, resulted in partition of Ireland in 1921. Violence gave birth to two confessional states and violence continued to dominate the new Northern Ireland, eventually leading to the most recent phase of sustained violence in 1969.

The wars of religion in the seventeenth century had a wider European context. The 1798 Rising, with its emphasis on justice and equality, was heavily influenced by the French Revolution and the American War of Independence. The Ulster Unionist resistance of 1912 was being religiously shaped by empire theology and politically determined by the Protestant sense of belonging to a British Empire, with the Bible assuring its greatness. The Easter Rising occurred in the context of the Great War when blood sacrifice for the sake of a nation was a pervasive ideology and the freedom of small nations, like Belgium, was a core cause for going to war. In a very real sense none of this violent Irish history occurred in a narrow Irish context but was being shaped and influenced by larger European and global events.

Underlying the pattern of violence in Irish history is the myth of redemptive violence, which has its roots in the ancient Babylonian myth from around the twelfth century BCE. In essence the myth declares that violence achieves, defends or saves. It asserts that war is necessary for peace and violent victory is necessary for security. It is the myth that underpins ancient Irish stories, such as those of CuChulainn and the Fenian Cycle. It also underpins national security policies and contemporary electronic war games and violent movies. The myth of redemptive violence underlies the history of British policy in Ireland and Republican and Loyalist violence.

This myth has dominated Irish thinking for centuries. The physical force tradition, which resurfaced when a constitutional approach to political negotiation failed, or faltered, is founded upon it. Those who have embraced the myth are convinced that the only way to peace is heightened security, private armies to protect particular interests, and separation from the perceived enemy. The cycle of violence will only be broken when the false premise, on which the myth is based, is exposed and rejected; and people are convinced that consensual politics and active nonviolent strategies for peace are effective.

Our theological dogmas and beliefs influence our sociopolitical and economic praxis, and vice versa. Our God-images, in fact, say more about the nature of the community holding them than they can ever say about the nature of God. Violent, vengeful, punishing god-images have predominated in the Irish religious landscape. These have reinforced a punitive view of justice, in both Catholic and Protestant communities, that is retributive and dehumanising, and translates into the need for private, paramilitary armies. This has also contributed to an increase in support for absolutist political parties. Instead of a theology of power, which is concerned with control and hegemony, what is required to build peace is an alternative model that validates power-sharing, flexibility and openness toward the other.

Sectarianism
Violence in Ireland since the seventeenth century has been overtly sectarian. Another way of expressing the same is to say, violence

has been expressed and experienced by people in Ireland as a form of sectarianism. But what is sectarianism and how has it impacted church and theology?

The Irish School of Ecumenics conducted a major research project between 1995 and 2000 on the role of Christian religion in sectarianism in Northern Ireland. A definition of sectarianism emerged from the research that focused on the intentions behind sectarian acts and the consequences for relationships. It stated:

> Sectarianism is a system of attitudes, actions, beliefs, and structures, which arises as a distorted expression of positive human needs especially for belonging, identity, and the free expression of difference and is expressed in destructive patterns of relating.[2]

The research underlined that sectarianism can work at personal, communal and institutional levels, that it always has a religious basis, and may involve a negative mixing of religion and politics. Listed as examples of destructive patterns of relating are: the hardening of boundaries between groups; overlooking others; belittling, dehumanising or demonising others; justifying or collaborating in the domination of others; and physically or verbally intimidating or attacking others.[3]

There is a plethora of examples in Irish history to support the Liechty–Clegg thesis that sectarianism is the consequence of the destructive blending of religion and politics. The partition of Ireland and creation of the Northern Ireland state were brought about by sectarian violence. As part of partition a PR (proportional representation) voting system was agreed for Northern Ireland in 1920 to ensure there would be a proportional representation of minority Catholic Nationalists in a Protestant Unionist majority state. However, Sir James Craig, the first Prime Minster of Northern Ireland, abolished PR in 1922 in local government elections and a few years later also abolished this

2. Joseph Liechty and Cecelia Clegg, *Moving Beyond Sectarianism: Religion, Conflict, and Reconciliation in Northern Ireland* (Dublin: The Columba Press, 2001), pp. 102–3.
3. *Ibid.*, p. 103.

method in Northern Ireland government elections. A Boundary Commission was ignored by Nationalists to their cost. Craig never really wanted it anyway and the Commission collapsed in 1925, creating Nationalist resentment and much unfinished business. The partition of Ireland did not create sectarianism but was the result of it.

An early attempt by the new Minister for Education to introduce a more integrated Education Bill was strongly opposed by the Orange Order and all of the churches. The Orange Order and the Protestant churches were insisting on their own particular interpretation of the Bible being part of the school curriculum. The Catholic Church feared the interference of Orangeism in its education system. The Bill was rejected and a sectarian educational system was built into the new Northern Ireland state from the beginning.

Divisive and exclusive sectarianism was not new to the northeast of Ireland. Sectarian agitation was present in the early eighteenth century, even though it was confined then to the divisions between the established Church of Ireland and Presbyterianism. Belfast itself was characterised by sectarian rioting since 1813. The next major incident was after 1825, 'but recent research in local newspapers and other detailed evidence has revealed that scarcely a year passed without provocation and violence of some sort'.[4]

The sectarian violence continued right through the early years of partition when over four hundred people in Belfast were killed, the majority being Catholic. Lisburn also experienced sectarian violence. In 1920, following the IRA killing of an RIC District Inspector and a Banbridge former Lieutenant Colonel, the towns of Banbridge, Dromore and Lisburn erupted in anti-Catholic violence. Especially in Lisburn, Catholic businesses and homes were torched and families forced to flee. Despite arrests no one was ever charged and only months after the end of sectarian violence in Lisburn 'civic leaders were once again threatening to use force to ensure Loyalist domination in the town'.[5]

---

4. Maguire, *Belfast*, p. 68.
5. Pearse Lawlor, *The Burnings 1920* (Cork: Mercier Press, 2009), p. 214.

In the years of economic depression in the 1930s shared poverty and the potential for shared Catholic–Protestant action became the victim of a sectarian divide and rule policy by the Northern Ireland Unionist government. It was also in the 1930s that James Craig famously declared a 'Protestant parliament for a Protestant people' in response to Éamon de Valera's claim of a 'Catholic state for a Catholic people'. Not only did Ireland have two confessional states but the combination of religion and politics meant that both were rooted in sectarianism with a continuing legacy into the future.

Electoral boundaries were gerrymandered in Northern Ireland with the worst examples in Derry, Omagh and Lurgan. In locations like these the property vote also ensured that Unionists held power. The property vote meant that property owning individuals had multiple votes and since Protestants owned most of the property a Unionist majority was guaranteed. These examples of a sectarian state created by already existing sectarianism have their roots in religion, which itself had been sectarianised from an early stage in modern Irish history. According to Marianne Elliott, Catholics and Protestants, in their origin myths, developed and perpetuated a negative and stereotypical view of each other. Further, the religious basis of these myths accorded clerics in both traditions, 'more power than they should have had'.[6] What form did these origin myths take?

Modern day Nationalism is built on the myth that Catholics are the true Gael asserting their Irishness in the face of persecution and dispossession from foreign settlers and planters in the seventeenth and eighteenth centuries.[7] The Penal Laws (1695–1756) militated against the open practice of Catholicism, endorsing this myth. Elliott indicates that behind the laws lay a fear of Catholic disloyalty to the Protestant king and parliament. Consequently, 'if Catholics were submissive, they were tolerated.'[8]

---

6. Marianne Elliott, *When God Took Sides: Religion and Identity in Ireland: Unfinished History* (Oxford: Oxford University Press, 2009), p. 258.
7. *Ibid.*, p. 21.
8. *Ibid.*, p. 169.

With Catholic Emancipation in 1829, the Catholic Church and its people gained a new confidence in Ireland. The pope appointed Paul Cullen as Archbishop of Armagh in 1850 and he undertook a radical revitalisation of the church, convening a national synod to: strengthen the faith, spread devotion to the sacraments, define the duties of clerics, and affirm the authority of the bishop in each diocese. He also embarked on major church-building pro-grammes and promoted the importance of Catholic education.

This new-found confidence found expression in the promo-tion of a Gaelic heritage. The Gaelic League was founded to pro-mote the Irish language and the Gaelic Athletic Association for cultivation of sport. There was also a resurgence of interest in Ire-land's literary past led by W. B. Yeats, Lady Gregory and J. M. Synge. In 1905 Sinn Féin was founded to set up Irish alternatives to the British parliament and civil service. While these develop-ments, in themselves, were not sectarian, they reinforced the association of Irishness with the Gael, and by extension Catholic experience.

Protestant fear of the Catholic Church as an institution, and in particular the papacy, was reinforced in 1908 when the *Ne Temere* decree came into effect. It declared invalid mixed marriages of Catholics and Protestants, unless witnessed by a priest. An implicit understanding was that any children resulting from a mixed mar-riage would be brought up Catholic. This became problematic for Protestants in Ireland with the founding of the Free State after partition. In spite of a guarantee of religious equality in the Free State Constitution, the Catholic Church held a 'highly influential position in the state and its power continued to grow when the Free State became a republic'.[9] Catholic morality began to influ-ence legislation and those in political leadership affirmed their allegiance to the Catholic Church before all else. As de Valera put it, 'If all comes to all, I am a Catholic first.'

Catholic sectarianism reared its head again in the Republic of Ireland after Vatican II, this time out of joint with the efforts of the Catholic Church to promote ecumenism between Christians.

---

9. Michael Staunton, *The Illustrated Story of Christian Ireland From St Patrick to the Peace Process* (Dublin: Emerald Press, 2001), p. 147.

The Archbishop of Dublin, John Charles McQuaid's response to talk of Christian unity in 1966 was indicative of a sectarian bias born of experiences of oppression in Ireland:

> Non-Catholics represent to us the people who deliberately strove for centuries to destroy the one true Faith, who till very recently occupied the dominant position in our economic and cultural life and who today stand for the English remnant that still holds a very great share of the sources of economic life.[10]

Catholic sectarianism has been one of the factors influencing the decline of Protestants in the Republic of Ireland from 7% to around 3% since the founding of the Free State.

What about the Protestant origin myth? For Protestants in Ireland their identity lay in being God's chosen people amidst an inferior, barbarous, indolent Catholic population. Loyalty to God and crown were perceived as inseparable, two sides of the one coin. Elliott points up that this marriage of church and state was reinforced in the Reformation-inspired belief that 'subjects could not be loyal if not sharing the same religion as the ruler'.[11]

Some Protestants, resentful of the Catholic monopoly of the term 'Irish', traced their lineage back to the ancient *Ulaid*, a pre-Gaelic ruling dynasty, which gave Ulster its name. They sought to undermine the 'blow in' perspective and establish prior claim to the province.[12] In the early to mid-nineteenth century, when the privileged status of the Church of Ireland as state church, began to be questioned, members of that church put up an argument for being the true representatives of Irishness.[13]

Irish Protestantism was primarily influenced by early seventeenth century Calvinism and Puritanism, which considered Catholicism a tyrannical system rather than just a religion. It held

---

10. Elliott, *When God Took Sides*, p. 234.
11. *Ibid.*, p. 31.
12. *Ibid.*, p. 17.
13. *Ibid.*, p. 36.

Catholicism was governed by the dictates of a pope who was the incarnation of evil as described in the Bible.[14]

Popery was associated in the Protestant mindset with rebellion and persecution. The papal agenda was perceived as political, to establish a monolithic Catholic Church, and the Catholic religion itself viewed as reliant on superstition. Exaggerated reports of a massacre of Protestants in Wexford in 1798, led by a Catholic priest, Reverend John Murphy, and the alleged forced conversion of Protestants to Catholicism before they were killed, reinforced this perspective. Protestant memories of previous reprisals by Catholics on the Protestant community, in 1641 and 1689, were also stirred. And the belief that Catholicism was the antichrist plotting the extinction of Protestantism fuelled sectarian attitudes and actions.

Protestantism in Ireland was promoted as the antipathy of all things Catholic. Protestants perceived Catholic use of religious symbols as idolatrous, their beliefs as superstitious, their reliance on priests to mediate with God as error and their loyalty to the pope as a sign of disloyalty to the crown. Protestants believed themselves to have direct access to God, relying on the Bible as the only source of God's authority. They understood themselves as tolerant of others' religious and civil liberty, although this tolerance did not extend to those considered disloyal to the crown, which included Catholics. The Orange Order's perceived mission to 'combat popery and preserve the Protestant state', in Elliott's view emphasises the linkage between loyalty to Jesus Christ and loyalty to the crown in the Protestant mindset.[15]

The challenge for the churches, Catholic and Protestant, in Ireland is to help each other recognise the sectarian nature of their origin myths and in a new climate of reconciliation rethink exclusive and excluding doctrines and identities. A number of years ago the Irish School of Ecumenics Education for Reconciliation team facilitated a programme in Enniskillen looking at some of the doctrinal issues that divide the churches. Our concern was the impact

---

14. *Ibid.*, p. 53.
15. *Ibid.*, pp. 82–83.

of doctrines like 'Eucharist' and 'Justification by Faith' on rela-tionships. The focus was on recovering the relational and recon-ciling core of the Christian faith and not the confessional and divisive orthodoxy of belief. This also meant rethinking our ex-clusive truth claims.

Exclusive Truth Claims

The churches in Northern Ireland live in the past. They per-petuate, through their structures, dogmas and doctrines, a self-understanding and self-definition reminiscent of the sixteenth century divide between Protestant and Catholic churches, when each side claimed to be the true church. The institutionalising of difference that resulted from the Reformation, and which blinded each side 'to the truth in the other's position' has resulted in the nationalising of God, with both Catholics and Protestants in Northern Ireland claiming God on their side.[16] Certain theological propositions gave expression to exclusive truth claims.

1. *The one true church outside of which there is no salvation*

This exclusive claim was made by the Catholic Church until Vat-ican II when it was modified to declare that 'the unique church of Christ … subsists in the Catholic Church'. This was repeated in the document *Dominus Jesus*. The latter document did not refer to other Christian communities as churches but as 'ecclesial com-munities'. Apostolic succession and a valid Eucharist were said to constitute true particular churches. This excluded the signifi-cant Reformed and Pentecostal traditions and unsurprisingly was not well received. The questions remain: did the modification of Vatican II go far enough; and does 'the one true church outside of which there is no salvation' still exist in a modified but exclu-sive way?

The claim has not been the monopoly of the Catholic Church. Various expressions of evangelical faith have the same logic. In some cases, unless there is a particular and fundamentalist inter-

---

16. Gabriel Daly O.S.A., *One Church: Two Indispensable Values: Protestant Principle and Catholic Substance* (Dublin: Irish School of Ecumenics, 1998), p. 5.

pretation of scripture there is no authentic experience of salvation or faith.

2. *Error has no rights*

Beginning from propositional truth claims and confessional doctrinal formulations it is a small step to the exclusion of those who do not conform to the claims and formulations. Any deviation puts people outside the pale and they are considered to be in error. Error then has no rights, or lesser rights and a practice of separatism is developed to varying degrees. In the past this meant being burned at the stake but such actions in contemporary times would not be tolerated by a society that considers itself more civilised. However, metaphorical and all too real forms of exclusion are introduced. The literal stake can be replaced by social and political discrimination treating 'heretics' as second or third class citizens, excluding people from jobs, housing and basic civil rights. All theology, not least sectarian theology, translates into social and political policies.

Error has no rights reaches a logical conclusion in exclusion of 'the other' from the Eucharist, or 'the other' becomes the object of aggressive evangelism or conversionary tactics. Error has no rights leads to religious, social and political separatism and a superiority complex destructive of human and community relations.

The flip side of error has no rights is a distorted doctrine of providence, which would normally mean God's care for people, but which in a sectarian context slips into 'God is on our side'.

3. *Predestination and Election*

There is no question that these ideas are in the biblical text but the question is what interpretation has been imposed on them? The texts can be read as God's gracious choice of a people not for privilege but for the responsibility of being a particular light to all peoples. In this sense predestination and election are read as God's gracious empowerment of a people for a purpose but never as an excuse for privilege and superiority.

Another approach is to read these texts from the perspective of privilege. In the Irish context this was shaped by political realities. Calvin had read the texts in a legalistic way, imposing upon them a theology of double predestination where God had chosen some for salvation and others for damnation. Either way it was God's sovereign choice. The Anglican *Thirty-Nine Articles* had been influenced by Calvinistic theology but stopped short of double predestination. The Church of Ireland, not satisfied with thirty-nine articles, in the early seventeenth century produced one hundred and four. There were two main differences. To the earlier Anglican emphasis, that God had predestined some to salvation, the Irish added and predestined others to damnation. It was a doctrine of double predestination, which in fact was strictly Calvinist. This was a neat rationalisation of the failure in Ireland to convert Catholics to the true faith but it was theologically destructive of relationships. The other theological plank in the *One Hundred and Four Articles* was to describe the pope as antichrist. That too was a neat sectarian rationalisation of a minority community's historical experience. It was a rationalisation of failure.

In fairness, in a few years Irish Anglicans reverted to the *Thirty-Nine Articles*. The doctrine of double predestination though was expressed in the Presbyterian *Westminster Confession of Faith*, where the pope was also described as antichrist. Reformed theology was strictly Calvinist and whatever it meant in Geneva it took on a sharper edge in a sectarian context where both sides defined themselves in opposition to each other. Double predestination and election made historical and political sense to a settler community insecure in their close proximity to the Catholic Gael. The sectarianisation of theology means the politicisation of theology with destructive consequences for relationships in a contested space.

4. Petrine Ministry

Catholic theology also read the Bible in a politicised way, imposing a doctrine of apostolic succession on a single Matthean text: 'And I tell you, you are Peter, and on this rock I will build my church, and the gates of Hades will not prevail against it.' (Mt 16:18)

The interpretation of the text is disputed and different readings have been offered in a polemical context. Peter's name in Greek is *Petros* and the Greek for rock is *petra*. There is obviously a play on words but there the interpretations part company. Was the rock Peter, or Peter's confession of faith? Is the church built on Peter *per se*, or the faith that Peter confesses in response to Jesus' question in Matthew 16:13: 'Who do people say that the Son of Man is?' Peter's faith response was: 'You are the Messiah, the Son of the living God.' (Mt 16:16)

Historically the Catholic Church has placed the weight of interpretation on the person of Peter but the alternative reading is equally valid. Both ways, it is interpretation and there can be no certainty about either. The Catholic tradition has built a whole doctrine of apostolic succession on a proof text, which might be seen as a rather dubious way for Catholics or Protestants to read the Bible. Is it valid to place the weight of an entire doctrinal infrastructure on a single text? Furthermore, there is no historical evidence for an unbroken line of succession all the way back to Peter. There are in fact so many gaps in the succession that the doctrine may be no more than pious fiction. It may be that apostolic succession, like double predestination and election, are the inventions of political power bent on domination, which is hardly in keeping with Paul's kenotic theology in Philippians 2, or the prevalent servant image of Christ.

The proof text approach can be described as bibliolatry, 'an excessive adherence to the literal interpretation of the Bible also known as fundamentalism'.[17] This has generally been characteristic of Protestant fundamentalism but Catholic traditionalists and Protestant fundamentalists mirror each other. The Council of Trent affirmed that the one God is author of both Testaments as well as, 'The tradition concerning both faith and conduct … which had been preserved in unbroken sequence in the Catholic Church.' To this quote from the Council, Gritsch comments, 'Here, biblical and traditionalist fundamentalism are united: both the canonical Bible and the tradition of the church are viewed as being verbally inspired.'[18] These mutually exclusive fundamentalisms produced the infallible Bible on the one hand and papal

---

17. Eric W. Gritsch, *Toxic Spirituality: Four Enduring Temptations of Christian Faith* (Minneapolis: Fortress Press, 2009), p. 45.
18. *Ibid.*, pp. 64–65.

infallibility on the other. Both are abuses of power, are sectarian in their consequences and are rightly described by Gritsch as 'toxic spirituality'.

Sectarian theology, which is exclusive and separatist theology, is ultimately based on a misuse of power. It is shaped by the need for power over, or power as domination of others and always translates into social and political relationships with destructive consequences. Sectarian theology becomes a domination system, which always is the antithesis of the gospel. A sectarian faith has failed the people of Northern Ireland, distorted the gospel and made the churches dysfunctional in the public place. It may well be that violence needs to be demythologised, sectarianism deconstructed and truth claims radically relativised, if there is to be a more authentic expression of faith on this island.

The next chapter will continue to explore the contemporary context for churches in Ireland from a more global perspective by focusing attention on the end of Christendom.

Questions for reflection:
1. What is the relationship between faith and politics in a pluralistic, participative democracy?
2. Did the modification of Vatican II go far enough and does *the one true church outside of which there is no salvation* still exist in a modified but exclusive way?
3. Can we move beyond divisive, sectarian interpretations of scripture and tradition to heal relationships and promote positive inter-church relations?

CHAPTER TWO

Living with the End of Christendom

Clovis was a king of the Franks who resisted his spouse's Christian faith. In 496 CE, when his soldiers were being slaughtered in battle, Clovis prayed to Jesus. His prayer was conditional. He would believe in Jesus if he was first saved from his enemies. The enemy fled and Clovis believed. When his soldiers also accepted Christianity he requested baptism and was baptised on Christmas Eve. Though he removed his armour for baptism, he entered the pool still wearing his helmet. Three thousand of his soldiers followed, establishing a pattern of collective baptism that became the norm in Western Europe. Believing in Jesus and having been baptised, Clovis proceeded to conquer Gaul and kill off every relative who might threaten his power.

Conversion, baptism and military conquest were the characteristics of this fifth-century Western Christian. Did he have a role model? His hero was Constantine who, along with his soldiers, also accepted the Christian faith in a military crisis and continued in his faith to conquer and dominate. The model Clovis adopted from Constantine 'reflected and shaped the vision and values that would be characteristic of Christendom in the West'.[1] The Christian God legitimised wars and conquest. Christianity and culture were identical. Faith and politics were intertwined and to be normal citizens of Gaul was to be Christian.

In July 1567 a child was crowned at Stirling as James VI of Scotland. The Bishop of Orkney performed the coronation while John Knox preached a thunderous sermon from the biblical book of 1 Kings. The king grew up a vicious character, drank too much and was given to indecent language, enjoying crude entertainments. Not unusual for monarchs, his homosexuality was public and widely known.

---

1. Alan Kreider, *The Change of Conversion and the Origin of Christendom* (Harrisburg: Trinity Press International, 1999), p. 88. The Clovis story is adapted from Kreider, pp. 86–88.

When James VI of Scotland became James I of England he produced the great Authorised Version of the Bible or the King James Version, much loved by English language purists and conservative and fundamentalist Christians. James had strong religious beliefs about kingship. Kings were ordained of God, not by humans. He was the Lord's anointed in an absolute way. It was only to the Almighty that the monarch was accountable for his actions. No parliament, Presbyterian General Assembly, or any human body had an authority over the king's actions. Such was James' belief in the divine right of kings. This theology of monarchy was only possible in the context of the Christendom model that became dominant in Europe after Constantine and Clovis.

James, however, ran into a major roadblock in Presbyterian Scotland. The General Assembly of 1560 had established Presbyterianism in Scotland as a church to be entirely free of royal decree, without bishops and with a very democratic form of church government. James hated Presbyterianism and had a number of confrontations with its leaders. Perhaps the most spectacular was with Andrew Melville. Melville's famous retort to James was devastating for one who was king by divine right:

> Thair is twa kings and twa Kingdoms in Scotland. Thair is Christ Jesus the King, and His Kingdome the Kirk, Whose subject king James the Saxt is, and of whose Kingdome nocht a king, nor a lord, nor a heid, but a member![2]

The Reformed Protestant tradition with its strong emphasis on democracy and decentralised power had the potential to be subversive of the Christendom model. It could radically undermine the divine right of kings, the marriage between throne and altar, church and state. But all the classical models of the Protestant Reformation failed in this. Christendom remained intact through its Roman Catholic and Protestant expressions. Even Melville was locked into the classic Christendom model when he identified God's kingdom with the kirk. In Presbyterianism there was no salvation outside the church. But God's kingdom has

---

2. John MacLeod, *Highlanders: A History of the Gaels* (London: Hodder and Stoughton, 1996), p. 111.

never been identified with the church, something Christendom could never see. Rather the kingdom of God was and is always larger and greater than the church and salvation has never been tied to church as institution. It is possible that the sixteenth century religio-political revolution eventually undermined Christendom and led to its demise, especially in the second half of the twentieth century.

The Origin of Christendom

There may well be three eras within the history of the Christian faith. They are:

1. Pre-Christendom
2. Christendom
3. Post-Christendom.

These do not represent three clear-cut eras. There is overlap with one era overrunning into the next. It would be naïve to think that in the post-Christendom era, Christendom is completely dead. Much of the religious right in the USA seems bent on maintaining it, even strengthening it. It is even possible that a new Christendom will or even is emerging on the African continent. Nor did pre-Christendom completely disappear after the fourth century.

For the first three centuries Christianity was a minority faith. Society around it largely ignored it or despised it. From time to time Christians suffered persecution, being scapegoated for the fire of Rome by Emperor Nero in the mid-first century. The Christian communities behind gospels and letters of the Christian Testament were very small. The recipients of Paul's letter to Thessalonica may not have numbered more than two dozen. The church was characterised by small house churches, a room in a tenement building or shop, or an occasional house owned by a wealthy Christian sponsor. This will be further explored in chapter 4.

The early experience of the church was as a minority movement, originally a Jewish Jesus movement and towards the latter part of the first century, a Gentile Jesus movement. By the time Paul wrote to the Roman and Corinthian house churches, they were mixed, and characterised by internal relational tensions rooted in ethnicity, gender and class. Development continued as did the tensions and conflict often in relation to power, authority and leadership. Overt power struggles are evident in the Pastoral letters of I and II Timothy and Titus with strong currents of cultural tension evident in Colossians and Ephesians, all of which belong to the end of the first century or even early second century. There is also a strong pacifist tradition in the church of the first three centuries with active non-violence and non-involvement in the military being characteristic.

More attention is now being given to the theology produced in this context in terms of how these early faith communities talked of God, Jesus and how they understood the church's purpose in the world. A major field of biblical studies is now empire studies, paying detailed attention to the immediate context, indeed foreground of the Christian Testament writings and experience of the early Christians. The Roman Empire with its ideology, some would say theology of empire, dominated everything. The pre-Christian era is now being seen as faith over against empire and Christian faith communities as subversive and alternative communities called to witness to God's alternative empire.

The theological world view of these early Christians is being given special attention today, not least because the minority, de-privileged status and critical alternative role reflects the experience of many Christians in today's Europe and world. However, the world view and theology was to change in the fourth century. Constantine, the Emperor, intervened and reshaped Christianity and its sacred texts.

Faith in the Service of Political Ambitions

The story of Constantine's conversion has often been told and is much debated. How authentic or deep was his conversion? The empire was in crisis with power insecurity shared between four 'emperors'. By mid-310 CE three of the four had died in humiliating circumstances. One died of a terrible disease, while Constantine forced another to hang himself after he discovered a plot to overthrow him. (Senior and junior emperors were not good for the empire!) Civil war loomed to determine who would rule the western part of the empire. Constantine felt that he needed supernatural assistance if he was to succeed, something more powerful than military forces. Just before a battle at Milvian Bridge, outside Rome, Constantine prayed to 'the god of his father'. At noon he saw a supernatural sign in the sky, or so he told the church historian Eusebius years after. It was a cross of light with the inscription, 'By this sign you will be victor.' During the night Christ appeared to him holding the same sign and telling Constantine to use the sign as protection in the battle. Next day his craftsman produced a gold cross, including a Christ symbol which was also painted on his soldiers' shields. The battle began and Constantine entered Rome in triumph, going straight to the palace to offer prayers to the Christian God. He immediately issued letters forbidding the persecution of Christians. In 313 CE he issued the Edict of Milan which allowed freedom of religion.

Whilst this Edict meant freedom of religion for all religions, the Christian faith was especially privileged. Clergy and churches were given special protection and church property was restored. The state now paid clergy their salaries and state monies built larger places of worship. Clergy were now salaried officials of the Roman Empire, church extension was state sponsored and it was decided that the Bishop of Rome should have a grander place in which to live. The voluntarism of the Pauline church disappeared and the Lateran Valle with its estates replaced the Christ who had 'nowhere to lay his head'. Imperial religion now needed a great temple to reflect its status and an imperial-style basilica; St John's Lateran Cathedral was built and became a model for grand church building programmes. 'Constantine and Catholic Christianity were now undisputed masters of the Roman Empire.'[3] God and empire were now one, a reality which changed theology and shaped the final form of the Christian Testament.

The peace of the empire was threatened by theological controversy. There was disagreement about the nature of Christ as second person of the Trinity. The controversy angered Constantine; after all the faith was supposed to cement the unity of his empire.

---

3. David R. Dungan, *Constantine's Bible: Politics and the Making of the New Testament* (London: SCM Press, 2006), p. 107.

Constantine ordered all the bishops to a general synod at Nicaea in modern Turkey. In Constantine's summer palace they met in June, 325 CE and the emperor took direct control of the conference and its agenda. The imperially controlled agreement became known as the Nicene Creed and Constantine's letter made it the law of the land. The unity of the empire needed uniformity of faith. Imperial religion had no room for diversity and the pejorative word 'heresy' entered the Christian vocabulary. Constantine's letter contained another harsh and far-reaching statement: 'Let us then have nothing in common with the detestable Jewish crowd, for we have received from our saviour a different way.' Even Jesus was no longer one of that 'detestable crowd'.[4] Constantine was now fully and deeply involved in the affairs of the church and the church was fully in the service of the empire.

By 321 CE he had standardised Christian worship by making the Roman Sun Day a legal day of rest. He sponsored an unprecedented building campaign. His mother Helena built two large basilicas, the Church of the Holy Sepulchre in Jerusalem and the Church of the Nativity in Bethlehem. Constantinople became the new Christian capital, the 'new Rome' and Constantine pursued methods of mass conversion.

After the council of Nicaea, Constantine issued an edict against heretics. The latter were known as 'pests of society', and were forbidden to ever meet, had their houses of worship and books destroyed, as the books belonging to these 'pests' appear to have been controversial. There were two major arguments going on. Which books were the authentic writings of the Apostles and what was the correct interpretation of them? Constantine closed down that lively and heated discussion, which was also a power struggle. Which group, books and interpretative methods would dominate the church, be the standard orthodoxy and maintain and strengthen the unity of the empire? Public debate over scripture was silenced, the heretics went underground and Eusebius was instructed to prepare without delay fifty copies of the sacred scriptures. The heavy-handed Constantine closed the

---

4. *Ibid.*, p. 113.

canon of scripture and imposed not so much the authorised version but the authorised interpretation. Orthodoxy was imposed.

The church of Jesus Christ, hailed as the Prince of Peace, 'was offered recourse to the imperial sword – and took it, gladly … now it could simply compel agreement and punish disagreement'.[5]

Leadership was now in the hands of power-hungry and greedy politicians and bishops. God and Jesus were constructed after the empire's image, diversity was stifled and critical voices silenced. The Jewish Jesus had become an imperial conqueror. Christendom was politically powerful and the church in structure, style, dress and practice became imperialistic. Constantine's successor, Theodosius, legalised the Christian faith making it the only legal religion in the empire and also declaring all other religions, including Judaism, illegal.

Characteristics of Christendom

Christendom has been characterised by particular traits and values. They are still recognisable in Catholicism and Protestantism, reflected in the institutions and in mindsets. Even though Christendom entered its death throes in the mid-twentieth century, these characteristics stubbornly live on.

Orthodox Christianity, the religion of society, became the enforced norm. Christian symbolism and rituals provide the ethos of the civil and political society. The system of orthodox beliefs must be adhered to with the wrath of the institution responding in different ways to those who step out of line, or are deemed unorthodox or heretical.

As indicated in chapter 1, error has no rights and heresy is not tolerated. In the fourth century heresy was outlawed and other religions banned. No rivals of truth are tolerated and unity as uniformity is supremely important. 'Religiously, a Christendom society is a one-party state.'[6]

All belong and everyone is a Christian. The use of the word 'parish' implies that all are parishioners, an implication not yet

---

5. *Ibid.*, p. 125.
6. Kreider, *Change of Conversion*, p. 92.

dead. Christian society is homogeneous and the presence of other faiths creates tensions and resentments. A Christian society is dominated by Christian symbols, rituals and holidays, even when a majority ignore them.

The church–state relationship is closely entwined. The church legitimises the state, especially its armies and wars and provides the rituals on state and military occasions without any critical awareness or evaluation of the kind of God that underpins these state liturgies. This is a two-way street as the church receives protection and privilege from the state and retains its role at the centre of society.

Clericalism has been a key characteristic of Christendom. Some Christians were professionalised and shaped their own hierarchy and elite separated by ordination, in some cases a sacrament, from the lower grade laity. Leadership and power as well as authority were vested in the professional clergy caste.

All of these characteristics are recognised throughout a millennium and a half of Christian history. Vestiges still remain and even refuse to go away despite the reality that the church is now in a very different world and context, especially in the West and North America.

From a theological perspective Christendom has had devastating effects. Not only did the Nicene Creed become a dominating norm, unique and unchangeable, thanks to the legal status Constantine gave it, closing down the canon of scripture and more importantly, narrowing down an authorised interpretation; it also put limits on the activity of the Spirit. Despite the Johannine Jesus promising the Spirit, who would lead us into truth, a Spirit who would have other things to teach us, the Spirit was now institutionally confined to orthodox dogma and institutionalised Christendom. With an ironic twist some speak of the Constantinian heresy, which is an imposed peace without orthodoxy.[7] In Christendom there is no place for God's future, God's not-yet. The kingdom or reign of God, which has yet to come in all its completeness, is minimised or deleted from Christendom. The

7. John Howard Yoder, *The Royal Priesthood: Essays Ecclesiological and Ecumenical* (Grand Rapids: Eerdmans, 1994), p. 152.

church has no critical, ethical voice because it has become identified with the world in mutual appraisal and support. The church has a vested interest in the systems of power and uses its theology and ritual to legitimise the order of things or the status quo.

Constantine and the Christendom model simply reflected the ancient Middle East model of the tribal deity. This was 'a god whose significance was not ethical but ceremonial'.[8] This tribal deity legitimises and blesses the national cause, the state arrangements of power even when unjust.

Eschatology, God's future dream, the fullness of the reign of God, ultimate justice, non-violence, love and peace is not pie in the sky escapism, but a critical judgement on the present and a radical alternative vision. In Christendom 'the church does not preach ethics, judgement, repentance, separation from the world; it dispenses sacraments and holds society together.'[9]

In abandoning eschatology the Christendom church abandoned the kingdom or reign of God, or identified it with the church, in Andrew Melville's case, with the kirk. Constantine replaced the universal reign of Christ with the universal reign of the empire. Only Christendom could have produced the crusades and George W. Bush's 'axis of evil'. The god of this religion blesses imperialism and nationalism and the reign of God is replaced by a specific state, nation or peoples' intentions, often the will to power as expansionism or domination. The god of Christendom may be the worst form of idolatry; and for over seventeen hundred years in the West the church has been happy to worship the almighty or emperor god, and in his (*sic*) name bless the state, its injustices, violence and wars.

The End of Christendom

As Europeans born in the twentieth century we have lived through another epochal shift. Not only do we belong to the bloodiest century in human history when our technological sophistication wiped out millions of human beings and destroyed vast tracts of the earth, we have also lived through the death of

---

8. *Ibid.*, p. 153.
9. *Ibid.*, p. 154.

Christendom. To be sure, our mass killing made a large contribution to Christendom's death. Our Eurocentric tribal deity died in the trenches, during the fire-bombing and the atomic destruction of two Japanese cities. We have lived through a cultural death of God. Perhaps with considerable clarity Nietzsche saw it coming. Was he really an atheist or was he reading the signs of the times? He was profoundly concerned by the meaningless abyss and nihilism that would be left by the death of this cultural deity. That marks him out as a more profound and careful thinker than many of today's new atheists. He was prepared to intellectually go where today's atheistic fundamentalists lack the courage to go.

It is not just the tribal deity of Christendom that has died, it is the death of a world view, a set of assumptions about Christian faith, a way of perceiving God, Jesus and the Spirit and a way of being church. The death of Christendom breaks open all of these things, shatters our models of power, authority and leadership, and is experienced as a kind of ecclesial future-shock. After all, Christendom outlived, or was around longer, than all the great empires. It saw off the Roman Empire that gave it birth and even though it was heartily embraced by the Portuguese, Spanish, British, Russian and other European empires, it was more enduring than all of them. When the end comes it is a trauma of major proportions. It is a future-shock which the churches have not yet critically evaluated.

The death of Christendom was on its way long before the mid-twentieth century. The sickness had set in by the eighteenth century. Something was shifting and new attitudes were in the making. A process of secularisation was underway. The French Revolution blasted a gaping hole in the ship of Christendom. The god of absolute power, monarchy and a politicised, wealthy church was badly wounded and perhaps never recovered. The twentieth century witnessed the acceleration of secularism, pluralism and the cultural disestablishment or de-privileging of institutional Christianity. If the broad theme of Christendom was to 'church' the whole world, authorised by Jesus himself, other faiths are wrong, even evil, at best respected but ultimately only a step on the way, requiring fulfilment in Christ. Humanity and nature was also understood as separate; it was humanity's God-given mandate to dominate and conquer the natural world. The death of Christendom depletes these attitudes. Post-Christendom is characterised by widespread secularism and religious plural-ism. Part of the future shock is that God may be dynamically pres-ent in both secularism and religious pluralism. It means that we have got to talk about and experience God in different ways, as a larger God-vision.

Secularism for the institutional church means a radical shift in its relationship to power. In Christendom it was too closely related to the centres of political power. In the secularism of the West, church is decentred, marginalised and finds itself on the periph-ery. The felt-experience is often that of exclusion, no longer calling the moral tune and with no automatic guaranteed right to be heard. Christendom meant either politically established or cult-urally established. But the state churches of Europe, including the Anglican Church in England, are no longer where they once were. The debate concerning the reduction in the numbers of Anglican bishops sitting in the House of Lords – currently twenty-six – and inclusion of representatives of other Christian denominations and World Faiths reflects the changing multi-faith and cultural land-scape. In the West, Christendom is in a state of decomposition, better described as cultural disestablishment.

Ireland has not had a state church since William Gladstone disestablished the Church of Ireland in 1869. Cardinal Paul Cullen was opposed to the political establishment of the Irish Roman Catholic Church, yet for much of the twentieth century the four larger Irish churches enjoyed cultural establishment. This is no longer the case with their cultural disestablishment becoming ob-vious during the last two decades of the twentieth century. The Western experience finally arrived in Ireland, brought about by increasing globalisation, growing plurality, economic depression, political scandal, and ecclesial abuse of children and the complic-ity of Christian churches in sectarianism and the violence that characterised it. Numerical decline is one outcome, but so too is the loss of power, status and influence in social and political so-ciety.

The church laments secularism, complains about what it sees as constant criticism and cynicism, and becomes increasingly defensive. The defensiveness betrays a sense of the loss of power, angst about the unreality of its religious assumptions and beliefs and the threat to its own structures of authority and leadership. A loud, promotional Christianity is not a sign of clarity and confidence but a real indicator of the demise of Christendom.

Religious pluralism has also ensured the death of Christendom. For most of church history in the West the reality has been a Christian hegemony. The church monopolised public space and its very public symbols and rituals were unquestioned. The church's theology and practice was rarely open to question. Theological and moral dogmatism was proclaimed with no one answering back, an absolute authority defining an absolute and exclusive truth. In that context obedience was expected and assumed. It was easy to proclaim and believe that Christianity was the only true religion, Jesus was the only way to God, salvation and the church was the kingdom of God and the only institution by which participation was possible.

Globalisation, increasing and unprecedented communication and information and the unlimited opportunities to travel, as well as global migration, has made religious pluralism the great reality of our time, displacing religious hegemony. Locally and globally neighbour religions live side by side. There is no escaping the goodness, truth and holiness of the other, not unless we bury our heads in the sand and go into a serious bout of denial. Unless we completely shut down our minds, we have at least nagging doubts about our absolute and exclusive truth-claims.

We now share religious space, which may leave us uncomfortable because it might mean sharing God and God's salvation, or purpose, for human flourishing and well-being. Christendom with its totalising claims and monopoly of sacred space is no longer true of the West. It was in the old German Democratic Republic, in the days of the Cold War, at the beginning of the second half of the twentieth century, that one Günter Jacob saw what was taking place. 'We are living at the end of the Constantinian era.'[10]

10. Quoted in John Douglas Hall, *Thinking the Faith: Christian Theology in a North American Context* (Minneapolis: Fortress Press, 1991), p. 204.

Remarkably he said that thirty years before the collapse of the Berlin Wall and the largely non-violent revolution that took place in Eastern and Central Europe.

Paradoxical as it is, secularism and religious pluralism have brought the Constantinian era to an end during the second half of the twentieth century. Of course vestiges live on and much Western church leadership wants to hold on to trappings of former power. Much of it is pretend and a delusion with serious consequences. Presumption upon the past power and glory of Christendom is perhaps the greatest deterrent to faith's real confession in our present historical context.[11]

The lack of awareness, denial or failure to critically evaluate and reflect theologically, is a blockage to authentic and humble witness in the present.

> The single most far-reaching ecclesiastical factor conditioning theological reflection in our time is the effective disestablishment of the Christian religion in the Western world by secular, political and alternative religious forces.[12]

It is a factor more far-reaching than the Protestant Reformations of the sixteenth century, a traumatic reality for those Protestants who seem to have more faith in the events of that time than in the living God. Apart from the radical Reformation and most of the Anabaptists, the classical Reformers assumed the Constantinian form of church, which was its serious fault line. Whether this epochal shift, comparable only to the shift that followed Constantine's Edict of Milan in 313 CE, is currently conditioning theological reflection, is open to question. There are few signs in Ireland that we are ready to do theology, shape our ecclesial structures of power, authority and leadership for a post-Christendom era. Chapter 8 will elucidate some of these signs. However, we have hardly recognised that our reading of the Bible is conditioned and shaped by Constantinian or Christendom hermeneutics. Whether fundamentalist, so-called conservative or liberal,

---

11. John Douglas Hall, *The End of Christendom and the Future of Christianity* (Pennsylvania: Trinity Press International, 1997), p. 3.
12. Hall, *Thinking the Faith*, p. 201.

evangelical or modernist, our reading lens are coloured by the
marriage of church and empire, and by over a millennium and a
half of nurturing in this culture. Our ecclesial and theological assumptions, structures of power, methods of biblical interpretation
and reading are deeply entrenched in Christendom.

> What we are witnessing (and to some degree participating
> in) is nothing less than a radical re-formation/purification
> of Christianity, comparable in magnitude only to the alter-
> ation which occurred at the other end of the same process,
> when the church moved into Caesar's court.[13]

Having now moved out of Caesar's court or been pushed, it
may well take the rest of the twenty-first century to articulate radically new expressions of theology and church for the post-
Christendom era.

Biblical Resources for Post-Christendom
Constantine not only heavily influenced the canon of scripture,
he also imposed a method of interpretation. Scripture was read
through the lens of empire producing a right royal theology. God
became the supreme monarch with a hierarchy of power relations
in a privileged church. Scripture was read in such a way as to support all of this. Constantine's Bible provided resources for Christendom. With that era at an end, can the same sacred text provide
resources for post-Christendom?

The challenge now is to read the Bible in a different way, using
a different reading strategy and method of interpretation. Not all
will want to acknowledge that the Bible always requires interpretation; there are those who will want to insist that it simply or literally says. What it simply or literally says may conveniently be
identical with Christendom, continuing to prop it up, or preserve
another status quo arrangement of power. Christendom meant
privilege and status for the church and its authority carried the
day in understanding God, Christ and Spirit and provided the
authoritative interpretation of scripture.

Post-Christendom means there is no longer a privileged claim.
There is a loss of institutional power and the steady erosion of the

13. *Ibid.*, p. 204.

social authority of clergy, pastors and priests. Not only the church, but many forms of external authority have been questioned and rejected in our time. The monarchical image of God as ultimate and absolute authority has also been rejected. Post-Christendom means that we have experienced the 'dethroning of Christian privilege'.[14] Few contemporary biblical scholars have grasped this better than Brueggemann, whose writings constantly engage with the challenge to interpret the text in a new and radically different context. He has faced up to the reality that 'proclamation of the gospel is no longer a privileged claim'. It is rather 'de-privileged communication'.[15] Truth in today's world is greatly contested, 'the truth about the reality and character of God and the consequent reality and character of the world'.[16]

It is at this point in the Hebrew Scriptures that Walter Brueggemann finds the most profound resource for a post-Christendom situation. Israel's story is precisely one of de-privileged communication. From Genesis to Malachi, the community of faith lives under the domination of successive empires. 'Either way as peasants or as exiles, Israel lives a great distance from the great hegemonic seats of power and the great centres of intellectual-theological certitude.'[17] All Israel can do is tell its story, give testimony in the great courtroom of public opinion. Proclamation smacks of certitude, absoluteness, and the assumption of being heard without question. But Israel gives testimony in the public court and makes a bid for assent. There is no guarantee in the hegemonic world of empire that Israel's testimony will be heard, still less accepted. It is the empire, or the domination system, that determines and imposes the reality and character of the world. What else were the Babylonian, Roman, British and American empires about? What is globalisation doing? What is the core thread of the Hebrew Scriptures, but 'essentially de-privileged testimony

---

14. Walter Brueggemann, *The Word Militant: Preaching a Decentering Word* (Minneapolis: Fortress Press, 2007), p. 123.
15. *Ibid.*, p. 122.
16. *Ibid.*, p. 123.
17. *Ibid.*, p. 125.

that construes the world alternatively'.[18] Israel's testimony is the 'testimony of alternative truth'.[19] In the face of empire, super-power, domination system, Israel gives testimony to a different truth, a very different view of reality and a radically different way of being human and whole in the world. Testimony, dispute, advocacy are Israel's voice in the public courtroom. The same situation is reflected in the Christian Testament, 'evident in Paul's testimony before imperial officials in the book of Acts'.[20]

In a post-Christendom world we need to read the Judeo-Christian Scriptures in their context, against the imperial, power as domination grain. This means reading the Bible as subversive, counter-testimony. It is a post-Christendom book more than it was ever a Christendom one. We may have a great deal to unlearn but in the process we can discover an empowering resource for the post-Christendom, de-privileged context in which we now find ourselves. In the poetry of Second Isaiah (chapters 40–55) we hear the Babylonian empire imposing its proclamation, its absolute truth and reality about its gods and the world. We also hear in the imaginary courtroom scenes Israel's de-privileged testimony, 'the testimony to be given by Israel, for a counter-truth about a counter-God with a counter-ethic in the world'.[21]

With such an energising and empowering resource through the art of reading the text against the empire, we can welcome the death of Christendom, the end of the Constantinian era, because being de-privileged means being free. We are free to recover and re-articulate a more critical testimony, a more prophetic word, which critiques the present and envisions an alternative world. We are free to reshape power, authority, leadership and church in ways more true to the faith than Christendom ever was. In the

---

18. *Ibid.*, p. 125.
19. *Ibid.*, p. 126. Brueggemann's major work on the theology of the Old Testament is a massive treatment of this theme, providing a key interpretative method for reading scripture in a post-Christendom and post-modern context. *Theology of the Old Testament: Testimony, Dispute, Advocacy* (Minneapolis, Fortress Press, 1997).
20. Brueggemann, *The Word Militant*, p. 197.
21. *Ibid.*, p. 128.

twenty-first century we are free 'because we need no longer carry water for the empire as was a given in a previous power arrangement'.[22] We shall explore the biblical exilic paradigm in more depth in the next chapter.

Questions for Reflection

1. If the pre-Christian era is now being seen as faith over against empire and Christian faith communities as subversive and alternative communities called to witness to God's alternative empire, what challenge does this present to churches today?

2. Do the churches interpret the canon of scripture from a Christendom world view? What difference would a post-Christendom interpretation make to our understanding of the Christian texts?

3. How do you understand John Howard Yoder's comment that in Christendom 'the church does not preach ethics, judgement, repentance, separation from the world; it dispenses sacraments and holds society together'?

---

22. *Ibid.*, p. 130.

CHAPTER THREE

The Hebrew Scriptures: Fashioned by Exile

A Christian Exile

The Christian Church is at a point in its history where 'God appears to be terminating our known world and inviting us to a new world in which the true nature of church and its mission can be recovered'.[1] The end of Christendom, collapse of modernity and growing secularisation has created an inhospitable environment for God-talk. The church has lost its power in the public place to influence policy and in Northern Ireland its moral authority has diminished in the wake of the abuse scandals and political revelations.

A fundamentalist, conservative Protestant may interpret the decline in church membership and the antipathy to religion in society as a consequence of unfaithfulness. The gospel has not been preached and tolerance toward a liberal, even ecumenical, perspective has resulted in a loss of standards. She/he will point to congregations which have increased in numbers because they have maintained a purity of belief and practice and avoided the wrath of God. The way forward, therefore, is to uphold a theology of separatism because 'Light cannot have fellowship with darkness'.

Another negative response that can be found across mainstream churches, Catholic and Protestant, is to deny that there is any breakdown in theocracy or moral authority. Adherents of this view admit that while there is evidence of some personal failures and glitches on the faith journey there is no crisis of belief or failure of church systems. The way forward is to carry on business as usual. Critiques of church by society, or the media, are met with a show of defensiveness and barriers are erected to protect the institution. This hyper-defensiveness also leads to separatism and

---

1. Paul D. Hanson, *The People Called: The Growth of Community in the Bible* (San Francisco: Harper & Row, 1987), p. 224.

similarly births a more conservative, fundamentalist, even aggressive belief system. Walter Brueggemann critiques the separatist reaction as a failure to understand and live out our baptismal call:

> Baptismal identity is not designed for ghetto existence. It is rather intended for full participation in the life of the dominant culture, albeit with a sense of subversiveness. There is no 'separate peace' for exiles, no private deals with God, no permitted withdrawal from the affairs of empire.[2]

There is no exact parallel between Judah's experience of exile and the churches' loss of power and status due to the death of Christendom.; however, the Israelites' response to exile in Babylon is instructive for those of us grappling with feelings of dislocation and displacement in the Christian churches in Ireland.

The Hebrew Bible evidences that the exile shaped Israel's understanding of itself as a people, and its relationship with Yahweh, more profoundly than any other event in its history. Exile was about the collapse of the small kingdom of Judah's politics, economics, social life, community infrastructure, moral maps and spiritual experience. Traditional faith was shattered, as was the world view and traditional God images. Exile, therefore, becomes a metaphor for any comparable loss of meaning, tradition, symbols and power. While Christians reading the exilic texts need to respect the integrity of the Israelite experience and avoid drawing easy analogies with the crisis in the Western church, we can learn something about processing pain, reformulating our faith in radical ways and strategising for survival as an alternative community.

One of the difficulties Christians in Ireland immediately encounter when faced with the task of engaging with the Hebrew exilic experience is how to read and make sense of it. Is there a right way of reading the Bible?

---

2. Walter Brueggemann, *Cadences of Home: Preaching among Exiles* (Louisville: Westminster John Knox Press, 1997), p. 13.

Reading the Bible in Ireland

> And when the Lord your God gives them over to you and you defeat them, then you must utterly destroy them. Make no covenant with them and show them no mercy.
>
> *(Deut 7:2)*

This text appeared on a wall mural in South Belfast. It was put there by Loyalist paramilitaries who obviously found in it the justification for killing enemies and remaining separate from them. It was a gable wall proof text, with no attention paid to literary and historical context. It represented a literalist reading of the Bible with violent sociopolitical implications. In Northern Ireland there is an over-reliance on a literalist, scholastic approach to biblical interpretation in both Protestant and Catholic churches. These interpretations often justify sectarian, sociopolitical and religious separatism. Texts without contexts can be used to justify anything, even murder.

There are a number of reasons why church congregations in Northern Ireland have lost sight of the surplus of meaning in the biblical poetry and myth and ignored the contextualised nature of the words and narratives. Firstly, a belief in the factual nature of the biblical text draws on an empirical research methodology believed to verify these facts. Such a world view has its roots in the nineteenth-century scientific objectivist illusion that was incapable of recognising that all facts are, in reality, interpretations. Secondly, this perspective also holds that what is factually true is also historically true. Thirdly, added to this is a view of divine inspiration that believes the Bible is literally, factually, and historically the Word of God; that in truth God dictated the words of scripture. Finally, any other strategy for reading scripture, which does not fit with this theory of inspiration and revelation, is rejected as untrue. In reality what this means is that the word of God serves a male, patriarchal, hierarchical, status quo social order and praxis.

The mainstream Protestant churches in Ireland also read scripture through other interpretative lens. Church of Ireland theology has been shaped by the *Thirty-Nine Articles*, which is mildly

Calvinist. The Church of Ireland is also shaped by its Irish context, in which it is largely a low-church form of Anglicanism. This is a reaction to Irish Catholicism. In the Presbyterian Church the *Westminster Confession of Faith*, although described as 'a subordinate standard', nevertheless is the Calvinistic filter through which many Presbyterians in Ireland process and understand theology. Methodism in Ireland has been shaped by an Irish interpretation of Wesley's theology. Methodist ministers are required to read Wesley's *Standard Forty-Four Sermons* and his *Explanatory Notes on the New Testament*. They are meant to provide a theological template for interpreting scripture and applying it, they capture the ethos of Methodism summed up in the doctrine of holiness. But Wesley has been filtered through a pre-critical conservative, fundamentalist system. In each of these churches, while the standards are external to Ireland, they have been interpreted within a historical sectarian context. Certain anti-Catholic themes can be emphasised in all three standards. The standards by which scripture is read are pre-critical and largely pre-modern.[3]

Prior to Vatican II the Catholic Church read the Bible from the perspective of 'tradition'. It, too, read the Bible from a pre-critical perspective, which was literal and flat. At Vatican II the Catholic Church entered into the modern world and began to read the Bible from the perspective of historical criticism. This entailed

---

3. There are three different attitudes toward the Bible. 1) A pre-critical perspective assumes biblical texts are literally true. Those who read from this stance do not question the contradictions in the texts themselves. They believe there was a miraculous star in the night sky when Jesus was born, and that angels really did appear to shepherds to announce his birth. 2) A critical approach developed in the modern period, dating from the Enlightenment in 17th and 18th centuries up until mid-20th century. Adherrents asks questions of the biblical texts to discipher what is factully true; i.e. Did it happen this way? 3) A post-critical perspective sees the truth in the biblical texts while admitting this truth does not depend on being factually or historically true. It appreciates that the writers used story-telling techniques to convey the truths of their faith. For instance, the star in Matthew's Infancy Narrative was the gospel writer's literary creation affirming Jesus as the light of the world.

engaging faith with the scientific world view. For instance, readings of Genesis began to pay attention to evolution and science.

The challenge for all the churches in Ireland, now, is that the world has moved from modernism to postmodernism, in which there is no master narrative, no objectivity, and a plurality of truths. The Western world has also moved beyond Christendom. So how do we read the Bible in a world where there are competing interpretations and world views and the monochrome premodern worlds of Trent, Calvin, Cranmer and Wesley do not exist anymore?

Not One Voice but Many

The Bible is a human product written by two communities, Ancient Israel and the early Christian movement. It is a literary response to the experience of God in these ancient communities. It is not a divine product, written from God's perspective, but it does take the reality of God seriously. The Hebrew Scriptures are, for the most part, a theological reflection on Israel's life with God in various imperial contexts.

The scripture texts reached their final canonical form post-exile. Brueggemann dates the completion of the Torah to the fifth century BCE, and the completion of the Prophets' corpus to the second century BCE.[4] Editors of the canonical texts had access to narratives and poems that were composed during the eighth and seventh centuries BCE, before the Babylonian exile. These compositions were redacted and added to during the exile by the elite who made up the literary minority. It is likely that the deportations acted as catalysts to goad scribes into gathering and preserving written documents. In fact, biblical scholars are increasingly recognising that the Hebrew Scriptures, in their final

---

4. Walter Brueggemann, *An Introduction to the Old Testament: The Canon and Christian Imagination* (London: Westminster John Knox Press, 2003), p. 5. The Torah consists of the first five books of the Bible; the Prophets include Joshua, Judges, Samuel, Kings, Isaiah, Jeremiah, Ezekiel, and the minor prophets; and the writings encompass Psalms, Job, Proverbs, Ruth, Esther, Ecclesiastes, Lamentations, the Song of Solomon, 1 & 2 Chronicles, Ezra, Nehemiah and Daniel.

form, are a product and response to exile in Babylon and that earlier materials, which predated exile, are given fresh interpretation in the exilic experience.

During the many editorial processes the biblical material went through before it reached its final canonical form there was no attempt to harmonise conflicting accounts. K. L. Noll sees this as evidence that: 'The motivation for the Torah's existence was one of preservation of variant traditions and not promotion of a single religious viewpoint.'[5] Consequently the Hebrew Scriptures witness to the plurality of interpretations concerning who God is and what it means to live faithfully the covenant relationship with God. These perspectives are often in dispute with one another, and occasionally one perspective prevails over the others. Yet the decision to let them sit side by side shows a readiness to respect counter voices and witnesses to the provisional nature of all God-talk, which if literalised, or taken as the final truth, becomes idolatrous.

As well as a diversity of voices within the biblical stories, there is now recognition of a plurality of perspectives on the meaning of these voices. It was the illusion of the Enlightenment that an interest free interpretation of the Bible was possible. Living as we do in a pluralist context, we can no longer ignore the diverse interpretations of biblical texts representing many different interests. Brueggemann advises that in this new reality:

> [The] honest facing of pluralism can only be pastorally and usefully engaged by truthful, respectful conversation. This means no participant seeking to 'convert' the other, and no participant knowing the outcome ahead of time. New 'truth' received together may well be out in front of any of us.[6]

All interpretations are provisional and always in need of revision. The Spirit of God is always ahead of us, enabling us to find

---

5. K. L. Noll, *Canaan and Israel in Antiquity: An Introduction* (London: Sheffield Academic Press, Imprint of Continuum International Publishing Group, 2001), p. 307.

6. Walter Brueggemann, *Cadences of Home*, p. 25.

fresh meaning in the biblical narratives for our time and context. There is never a final, authoritative interpretation. The enduring truth of scripture has always something new to say to us about how to live and how not to live.

Recent biblical scholarship has highlighted the importance of recognising the imperial context that formed the foreground to the Bible. From Genesis through to Revelation the dominating context is one successive empire after another. The history of Israel was shaped by the surrounding world of geopolitics and imperial expansionism. We cannot understand the Bible story, and in particular the story of Israel's exile in Babylon, in isolation from this imperial context.

In the Shadow of Empire

Like other small nations in the ancient Near East, Israel and Judah became pawns in the geopolitical manoeuvrings of rival empires seeking to dominate the Fertile Crescent, which linked Egypt to the West and Mesopotamia to the East. From the ninth century BCE onwards, except for a brief respite in the Maccabean period (165–63 BCE), when Israel again became an independent state, the Israelites were a colonised people. Noll dates the emergence of empires in the ancient Near East to the middle of the sixteenth century BCE when three rival powers Anatolia, Northern Mesopotamia and Egypt sought to control Syria-Palestine. Noll comments:

> Not only did this region offer natural resources of value … Syria-Palestine was also the land bridge that stood between the three powers. Each rival king desired control of that passageway, strategic both defensively and offensively, and each was willing to fight for it. Syria-Palestine became the battleground for the superpowers of the age.[7]

Syria-Palestine came under Egyptian imperial control from 1550 BCE until 1135 BCE. The decline of Egyptian power created the space for the resurgence of independent city-states in Syria-Palestine that had no centralised political structure. These

---

7. Noll, *Canaan and Israel*, p. 108.

flourished until the ninth century BCE, as deportees returned to their homeland and contributed to the rebuilding of the socio-economic and political infrastructure of a community destroyed by war and famine.

The geopolitical situation changed with the coming to power of the Assyrian king Tiglath-pileser III (745–727 BCE), who initiated a brutal expansion programme in Syria-Palestine resulting in the collapse of many small kingdoms. Israel and Judah were spared destruction but were forced to succumb and become vassal kingdoms.

Political instability often followed the death of an imperial ruler and upon the death of Tiglath-pileser III Israel rebelled against Assyria, along with other neighbouring kingdoms, hoping Assyria would be too unstable to take action. Israel was mistaken in its assessment and paid heavily for its disloyalty; it was invaded and destroyed by Shalmaneser V (727–722 BCE) and his successor Sargon II (722–705 BCE). In 721 BCE Israel's elite were sent into exile in another part of the Assyrian kingdom, and the remaining population forced into service in their former kingdom, now an Assyrian province.[8] This in effect wiped the northern kingdom of Israel off the map.

By 605 BCE a new Babylonian Empire was coming to prominence. The Southern kingdom of Judah found itself a vassal kingdom with a new Babylonian ruler, king Nebuchadnezzar II (605–562 BCE).[9] Judah, still somehow believing that it could gain its freedom from imperial control, rebelled against Nebuchadnezzar II and precipitated another attack on what was left of the kingdom.[10] This time Judah's king, Jehoiachin, was expelled to Babylon, along with members of the royal household, which included the priest and prophet Ezekiel. Nebuchadnezzar placed a new king, Zedekiah, on the throne, and the expectation was he would be loyal to Babylon. Judah, however, continued to involve

---

8. *Ibid.*, p. 219.

9. *Ibid.*, p. 219.

10. Judah believed that it stood a chance to gain freedom as Babylonian military forces had been weakened after a failed attempt to conquer Egypt.

itself in the geopolitical power struggles taking place in its midst, and when a new powerful king ascended the throne in Egypt, Judah believed the propaganda that Egypt would once again dominate Canaan. Zedekiah led a final rebellion, hoping for Egyptian military assistance that failed to materialise, and this time Nebuchadnezzar destroyed the kingdom, the city of Jerusalem, and the temple. In 587 BCE the elite of Judah were taken into exile, and Judah became a Babylonian province. There are no extant records indicating how many people lost their lives in this final siege.

From an imperial perspective deportation provided an economically viable option: it removed leadership from the kingdom, ensuring that the remaining population would be more easily controlled; and it exploited the talents of the elite in another realm of the empire. According to Noll:

> Deported Judahites maintained a community and an identity through the years of exile. They retained the worship of Yahweh and preserved some ancient writings that would become the nucleus around which the biblical anthology grew.[11]

What of the people left in Judah? Noll believes that life improved for those left behind, as they were allotted land to manage that was previously owned by the elite who were either killed or exiled. They also benefited from no longer having to pay a double tax, to the Judean king and Babylonian Empire, as the only authority they answered to in this new dispensation was Babylon.[12]

Fifty years after the first deportation of exiles to Babylon from Judah, Cyrus the Persian king (539–530 BCE) displaced Babylon as the superpower in the Ancient Near East. Cyrus, aware of the importance of good propaganda in managing a successful empire, presented himself as a liberator of exiles from Babylonian oppression. He also marketed his policy, to support the return of exiles to their homeland, as a magnanimous, humanitarian,

---

11. Noll, *Canaan and Israel*, p. 286.
12. *Ibid.*, p. 285.

imperial gesture. Gale Yee is, however, keen to explode this false impression by pointing out that this approach was part of a 'military strategy to strengthen and expand the imperial periphery'.[13] Cyrus also returned the treasures Nebuchadnezzar had removed from Jerusalem prior to destroying it, and promised financial support for the rebuilding of the temple. An expanded border, a repatriation of the exiled workforce to their homelands, and the establishment of a religious sanctuary, made sense economically. It provided an organised stable work pool to ensure the profitability of the land, an economic centre for the collection of tributes and taxes, and loyal subjects willing to defend Persia's interests against Egypt, and later Greece.

The elite in Judah benefited from the conflicts between Persia and the Egyptian and Greek Empires, as its positioning on the Western front meant the Persian king, Artaxerxes I (465–423 BCE), had to finance the rebuilding of Jerusalem's city walls. Without Persian state support the return of exiles, and rebuilding projects, would not have taken place. Those in Judah, who had not been in exile, generally opposed the Persian restructuring programme, as it created a priestly elite, who supported the status quo. Persia, however, went the way of previous empires and by 322 BCE it had been replaced on the world stage by the Greek Empire, which in turn gave way to the Roman Empire in 63 BCE.

The Catastrophe of Exile

The paradigmatic event for the Israelites was exile. In 586 BCE the Babylonians destroyed the original temple of Solomon and deported the ruling class of Judah to Babylon, bringing the Davidic dynasty to an end. The traumatic experience of exile shattered the Israelite world view. It was an experience of dislocation and deconstruction.

> They experienced a loss of the structured, reliable world that gave them meaning and coherence and found themselves in a context where their most treasured and

---

13. Gale A. Yee, *Poor Banished Children of Eve: Woman as Evil in the Hebrew Bible* (Minneapolis: Fortress Press, 2003), p. 137.

trusted symbols of faith were mocked, trivialised or dismissed.[14]

The prophets of the exile, in their efforts to make sense of this traumatic experience, evidence the existence of multiple interpretations that are indicative of disputatious world views. This is no 'one size' or a single outlook fits all. These competing perspectives also rely on very different images of God that have implications for Israel's future role as God's chosen people.

Jeremiah, a prophet of the exile, proclaimed the exile as God's punishment of the Israelites for breaking Yahweh's covenant. Their disobedience had angered Yahweh, who punished them using foreign empires to crush and destroy them (Jer 6:19, 23). Jeremiah aimed his invective at the elite in Judah, in particular the kings and those who had political power. Their self-interest and corruption influenced the policy decisions made at the expense of the poor and vulnerable. Jeremiah compares them to bad shepherds who have mismanaged and ill-served their flock (Jer 10:21). Their greed had caused them to act hastily, apparent in their challenge of Babylon, and readiness to trust in Egypt's military support. They have brought judgement, and terror, on themselves and on the nation. Their acts have consequences, judgement is effected; like 'reject silver' that has no purity or value they are to be tossed away (Jer 6:27–30). This rejection, however, is not ultimate. There is a way back through adherence to a 'new' covenant that has justice as its foundation stone. The prophets were not above using irony to drive their message home and in this instance Jeremiah is underlining the sad reality that had the covenant vision directed Israel's sociopolitical and economic relations and foreign policy the exile would not have occurred. The challenge is to recover covenant ethics and live by them.

Ezekiel, who trained as a temple priest, defined Israel's purpose as glorifying Yahweh by a life of holiness; he viewed the exile as a consequence of profaning 'my great name' (Ezek 36:22–23). For him, the exile was a purging experience, necessary for

---

14. Walter Brueggemann, *The Word Militant: Preaching A Decentering Word* (Minneapolis: Fortress Press, 2007), p. 113.

future faithfulness to Yahweh (Ezek 22:15). Ezekiel's vision of the valley of dry bones poignantly symbolises the departure of Yahweh from the temple and city of Jerusalem because of the people's depravity. What was required was the cleansing of the people and creation of a new heart and spirit (Ezek 36:26–27). In chapters 40–48 Ezekiel proclaims that the experience of exile would purify the people and prepare them to return home with a blueprint for rebuilding the temple and safeguards for preventing a future defilement (Ezek 43:6–9). For Ezekiel, 'everything depended on Yahweh's dwelling in the midst of the people'.[15]

A third major prophetic tradition that developed in exile and post-exile is found in Deutero-Isaiah (Is 40–55). This work anticipates the liberation of the exiles facilitated by the Persians, principally Cyrus II. Deutero-Isaiah predicts an end to the suffering of the Judahites in exile, as Yahweh, who is stronger than all other gods, will do 'a new thing' for Jerusalem (Is 43:19). The prophet reinterprets the monarchical almighty God-image, which had precedence in Judah prior to exile and was shattered in their conquest by Babylon. Yahweh instead is compared to a good shepherd, gently leading the flock home, caring for their needs, and carrying the young (Is 40:11). Yahweh's power, in contrast to the power displayed by empires, is rooted in mercy and justice.

In the context of exile the Israelites doubt God's capacity to care and remember and God's power to save. This leads to despair. Deutero-Isaiah challenges the exiles to remember Abraham and Sarah, who had faith that Yahweh would from them bring forth a people (Is 51:2). This defining memory is evoked to encourage exiles to believe 'in the power of God to work a newness' in their lives.[16] Similarly, the prophet recalls the memory of Sarah and Hagar to emphasise Sarah's despair at her barrenness, even though Yahweh had promised she would bear more children than Hagar. Like Sarah, the exiles are unable to see future possibilities and feel abandoned and bereft of hope. However, the new life promised to the exiles is beyond their wildest hopes and

---

15. Paul D. Hanson, *The People Called*, p. 222.
16. Brueggemann, *Cadences of Home*, p. 120.

imaginings (Is 54:1–3). Brueggemann points up that Deutero-Isaiah is inviting the exiles

> to sing against reality, to dance toward a future not even discernible, to praise the faithful God who will not be held captive by imperial reality. The singing, dancing, praising, is an act of hope, a betting on God's capacity for an inexplicable future.[17]

A third image, that of eating food provided by Yahweh, articulated in Isaiah 55:1–3, resonates with the manna story of Exodus 16. The alternative bread offered by Yahweh sustains the Israelites and provides nourishment, unlike the bread of empire which is used to coerce the hungry to submit to Egypt or Babylon.[18] The prophet calls the exiles to look to Yahweh for life, nourishment and hope, and not Babylon. Finally, Deutero-Isaiah also helps the exiles to reconstruct their purpose and mission. They are no longer to understand the covenant as an indicator of choseness and privilege, but as a sign of their responsibility, which is to be bringers of justice, 'a light to the peoples' (Is 51:4).

Priestly Perspective on Exile and Return
The priestly material, another strand of exilic writing inspired by Ezekiel and his followers, posited the future of Israel in terms of Yahweh's cultic presence. Like Ezekiel's visions, this perspective is a venture in hope, as the temple to which these writers appealed no longer existed. While Ezekiel emphasised the radical newness of Yahweh's intention to create within the exiles 'a new heart and spirit', the priestly writing underlined the faithfulness of Yahweh and 'the dependableness and perfection of the order established by God long ago, to which the people in exile could hope to return'.[19] They believed Yahweh was present in Babylon with the exiles. Yahweh was calling them to be a community of faith, in the midst of threats and danger, and would remain with them until they returned home.

---

17. *Ibid.*, p. 126.
18. *Ibid.*, pp. 129–131.
19. Hanson, *The People Called*, p. 224.

While in exile, the priestly writers developed a refined theology of sacrifice, related to atonement, which they gave expression to in Leviticus and Numbers. They believed that atonement would bring about the purity necessary for a right relationship with Yahweh. The sacrificial system and day of atonement were meant to maintain this state of purity.

> Through atonement, they hoped for the destruction of the chain of sin and death that held the community in bondage. Through atonement, a life-giving relationship with God could be renewed.[20]

The ultimate goal of the priestly system of sacrifice and atonement was that the community be brought into the realm of holiness. Holiness at least meant empowerment to keep God's commandments and live God's life. Much of this was understood as ritual purity, which in turn became an important identity marker for Israel. It was left to the prophets to give this key idea of purity a more ethical content. For the prophets holiness was justice.

In the post-exilic writings of the priest Ezra the Persian term 'Yehud' is used for the province and area that included Jerusalem, illustrating the power of imperial rulers to determine every aspect of the life of colonised nations, even their identity. According to the books of Ezra and Nehemiah, Ezra was commissioned by the Persian king to return to Yehud to instruct the people in the Torah of Moses, and Nehemiah was sent to rebuild the walls of Jerusalem and govern Yehud (Neh 12:26).

A characteristic of colonial governance was to encourage competition for financial or equivalent rewards between the elites in neighbouring colonies. The Persian government recognised the benefit of 'healthy' competition to the empire. Nehemiah opposed intermarriage with those from neighbouring areas to protect

---

20. *Ibid.*, p. 228. P is a traditional designation for the Priestly document. The other documentary strands in the Pentateuch are J (Jawhist), E (Eloist) and D (Deuteronomist). Scholarship has developed further substrands within these designations but JEDP remain the key identified strands.

Yehud from interference from officials representing the interests of neighbouring and competing colonies. Ezra's response was to instruct Yehudite men to divorce women they had married from neighbouring areas. His fear was twofold: that the purity of Israelite identity would be contaminated and that foreigners would inherit the Yehudite land and wealth.

Yee makes the point that the returning exiles had initially encouraged a pro-intermarriage policy to gain access to the land. These returning exiles justified this approach with an ideology that confirmed their status as the only 'true Israel' and, therefore, entitled to the land. This narrow ideological perspective provided for a categorising of people of the land as 'other' along with their foreign neighbours: Ammonites, Moabites and Edomites. This strategy also ensured control of Yehud would pass to the returning remnant or 'holy seed' (Ezra 9:2, 12).[21]

The change of attitude toward intermarriage, once control of the economy and resources was in the hands of the elite, likely created civil disturbance and righteous anger among the women and their extended families, who would have recognised the injustice of the decree on divorce. Ezra and Nehemiah justified their actions by appealing to the law of God. They reasoned the prohibition against intermarriage ensured the purity of their religious tradition that was in danger of being assimilated into a pluralistic culture and religious system. Yahweh is depicted as siding with the Yehud elite, supporting their pro-Persian and self-interested policies over against the poor majority.

Yet this exclusivist perspective, although dominant, was not the only one. The books of Ruth and Jonah are pieces of historical fiction set in the time of the Judges (eleventh century BCE) although written during the sixth and fifth century BCE by a Levite community returning from exile in Babylon. A key concern for the returning exiles was how to relate to the multicultural, multifaith groups, some of whom were historical enemies who had established themselves in Jerusalem when the majority of Jews were in exile. The Levites, who composed these books, put forward an

---

21. Yee, *Children of Eve*, p. 145.

alternative, radical and inclusive vision that challenges the priestly perspective. Consideration of Ruth's story evidences this.

Ruth, a Moabite, marries outside of her culture and religious tradition. As past relations between Moabites and Jews were antagonistic (Deut 23:3–6) there is cause to wonder how her family and community reacted to this interfaith marriage. Did their possible disapproval influence her decision to stay with Naomi, her mother-in-law, after the deaths of their respective husbands? In choosing to stay with Naomi, in spite of Naomi's reluctance and return with her to Bethlehem, Ruth challenges the rivalry and hostility between neighbour religions as well as the patriarchal system, which perpetuated the idea that life, and survival, depended on men. In Bethlehem Ruth took the initiative in creating the hybrid space to learn from Naomi the intricacies of the Jewish religion and culture, and her dialogue strategy furnished her with the information necessary to ensure their survival. In calling Boaz to honour his responsibility to her husband's memory by marrying her, as Jewish practice dictated, Ruth demonstrates how interreligious dialogue partners can assist those from neighbour religions to recognise and recover life-giving practices within their respective faith traditions. The holistic and liberating relationship that develops between Ruth and Naomi is cemented with the birth of Ruth's son.

The experience of exile has birthed at least two contrary responses. The priestly concern to rebuild a once great nation under Yahweh, with imperial support, is somewhat reminiscent of the pre-exilic stance. The Levite perspective demonstrates a radical shift in perceptions of God and choseness. The latter is closer to Deutero-Isaiah's understanding of tolerance toward others, which includes the responsibility to witness to God's compassion and justice for all.

As already indicated, our community praxis is closely tied to our image and experience of God. For the priestly cult, survival is about maintaining the traditions of the past that define and reinforce distinctive identity. For the Levites survival is dependent on the creation of relationships open to difference and otherness that recognises there is wisdom in learning how to relate interculturally.

Churches in Exile

The Israelites experienced first-hand the violence of empire as the Babylonian army swept through their land destroying lives, political, social and religious infrastructure and putting an end to their known world. It was a political and religious catastrophe. The Israelites survived and flourished because they engaged with what was going on, faced their pain, analysed their past and used imagination to reconstruct God, identity and purpose. Out of suffering and displacement they found fresh and divergent ways to articulate their faith, in all its struggle and promise.

This is the response required by churches in Ireland. The faith community needs to understand and acknowledge its loss of power and status and the seriousness of the crisis it now faces. Only when people of faith are able to own the inadequacy, and even collapse, of many traditional formulations of belief and practice can they begin to intentionally engage with the honest and painful deconstruction of these systems.

It was in exile that Israel's most creative and imaginative flourishing was experienced. The voices of lament, struggle and fear were articulated and heard. Anger at the brutality of the people's suffering was vented. Yahweh's faithfulness was remembered as stories from the past were recounted and reinterpreted. New theologies emerged, as the prophets sought to shape a new future from the past.

Who are the prophets in Ireland today? Are they in the churches, or on the edge of churches, even outside them? Perhaps they are to be found in all three arenas. Are we listening to the voices of suffering, struggle and hope within and outside the churches? Are we ready to engage and learn from the experiences of those who have been hurt and marginalised? How we respond to these critical voices and experiences will have implications for the way we, as church, live in community. What the Hebrew Scriptures affirm in the covenantal texts is that God's future is one where justice, compassion, truth and non-violence coexist at the heart of inclusive and hospitable community. Where these qualities are in evidence, God's presence is also to be found.

Irish churches engaging with reconstruction and re-visioning will not be able to do so without risks. The post-exilic story of return is full of tensions, as different groups competed to ensure that this or that vision of the future would be the norm. The priestly story shows that while it is important to remember and recover our particular religio-political identity and the responsibility attached to it, there is a danger if an emphasis on maintaining cultic purity results in a tacit legitimating of the social system at the expense of the poor and powerless. The stories concerning Ezra and Nehemiah also show how a theology of piety justified a social practice of separatism, with the introduction of the divorce law for exiles married to 'foreigners'.

The community experience in Northern Ireland has been largely one of segregation. This has found expression in education, housing, sport, as well as church, and the continuing difficulties around inter-church marriage. We may ask, whose system of purity is being maintained by all of this? Is sectarianism's insistence on maintaining a purity system and avoiding contamination from the other, an excuse for maintaining the status quo and protecting those who have power? Is this the system the churches are being called to give allegiance to or do we in fact need liberation from it?

The Levite response to religious and cultural difference is risky and may even be interpreted by some as 'letting the side down'. Engaging in honest dialogue with those outside of our own tradition can lead to reassessing traditional religious doctrines and practices. It can be an uncomfortable place to be. The Irish School of Ecumenics' commitment to creating opportunities for cross-community encounters in Northern Ireland is posited on the firm belief that the search for identity and truth takes place in the company of the other. When we move outside of our religious and sociopolitical comfort zones and form new relationships with those from different traditions, faiths and cultural backgrounds, we discover, in the words of the Jewish theologian, Emmanuel Levinas, that God is to be found in the 'face of the other'. In an Irish sectarian context this ecumenical approach offers a way forward for churches keen to connect with a pluralist culture and relate with neighbour religions.

A strong sense of religious identity can be enhanced by truthful and respectful engagement with the other. In fact, a commitment to deepening identity and faith is often the place from which informed dialogue begins, real listening occurs, and personal and communal enrichment happens. The Hebrew Scriptures confirm that faith and religious identity are impacted by context and similarly shape context. Faith that does not respond to and inform context is of no earthly good; in other words, it is failing to make real God's reign, or witness to God's alternative covenantal kingdom. Irish churches need each other to face up to and eradicate the sin of sectarianism and the religiously legitimised violence of our shared past. Unless the churches are transforming this dangerous and ungodly culture they are not only of no earthly good but religiously irrelevant and irreverent.

Exile and return provide models of contested stories as a faith community grapples with what it means to live faithfully in God's new vision for community. This exilic experience was not peculiar to the Israelites in ancient Israel. The early Christian communities were also places of exile from the dominant Roman culture and world view. The next chapter will engage with some of these exilic Christian communities to tease out the challenges and insights they present to Irish churches today.

Questions for reflection:
1. How do we read the Bible in a world where there are competing interpretations and world views?
2. How does a reading of the Exile story challenge contemporary Irish churches?
3. Is sectarianism at heart really an attempt to maintain purity systems and to avoid contamination from the other? Or is it a way of maintaining the status quo and protecting those who have power?

CHAPTER FOUR

Models of Church in the Christian Testament

No One True Church
Sometimes church communities in Northern Ireland claim there
is only one way to represent the true church; or a 'new' church
emerges alleging to have rediscovered the authentic Christian
Testament church. But there was no original church, or one true
church, and there was no uniform model of church.[1] Instead there
were a plethora of minority churches, often struggling for survival in antagonistic circumstances, attempting to hold together
their small congregations and live out their understanding of the
Christian gospel. These house churches were shaped and formed
in a variety of cultural, social and political milieu. The plurality
of models of church which evolved, each with its own struggle
and difficulty, were a response to the needs of the local contexts.

These house churches were generally in opposition to the
dominant Roman culture and the imperial world view, and this
left their members ostracised, and vulnerable to attack. Consequently, to be a Christian in the early church often meant living
in sociopolitical, religious and economic exile.

An in-depth study of some of the models of church that
evolved in the first century CE world of the early Christians can
inspire a rethinking of what it means to be church today. In this
chapter, five different ways of being church will be explored and
some of the challenges they present to Christians in this twenty-
first-century Irish context unpacked. A useful starting point is reflection on what Paul, and later Matthew, understood by church.

---

1. Paul S. Minear, *Images of the Church in the New Testament* (Cambridge:
James Clarke & Co., 1960, Reprinted 2007), p. 28; John Fuellenbach, *The
Kingdom of God: The Message of Jesus Today* (New York: Orbis Books, 1995),
p. 253. Minear conservatively estimates more than eighty models of
church but admits there may be up to one hundred. Fuellenbach settles
on the number ninety-five.

Paul's vision of Church

The primary term Paul used to refer to both the Christian movement as a whole, and the local house church communities, was
ekklesia. The word comes to Paul from the *Septuagint*, the Greek
translation of the Jewish Bible, where it referred to the 'assembly
of the Lord', the assembly of historical Israel. The Hebrew
equivalent *quhal* also meant the gathering of at least ten men 'for
prayer and worship' in the synagogue. In the Greco-Roman
world Paul inhabited *ekklesia* implied 'civic assembly', where political decisions about the well-being of community were made.
This assembly consisted of wealthy, male business people and
property owners, which generally excluded women and slaves
who were a sizeable constituency of any urban population. Paul
radicalised the word *ekklesia*. Working out of the Jewish tradition
in a Greek urban setting, he retained the idea of a gathered people
with responsibility for each other and for community. He rede-
fined this gathering as a worshipping, learning community with
ethical responsibilities for human well-being. It was no longer a
group of male elites. In Corinth and Galatia the *ekklesia* model was
a group of integrated people drawn from across classes and gender. It was a radical alternative to what was happening in the local
synagogue and city forum. *Ekklesia*, then, was a radical, alternative community to the Roman imperial order. The alternative society is rooted in the history of Israel, in opposition to the *Pax
Romana*.[2]

The churches, with which Paul and others were involved then,
were small communities of resistance at the heart of the military,
political and economic world of the Roman Empire. They were
not faith communities existing in isolation from the larger society,
whose faith in God was other-worldly. These were engaged communities, with much to say to us about how to be church and live
faithfully and ethically in the sociopolitical world.

---

2. Richard A. Horsley, 'Building An Alternative Society: An Introduction'
in *Paul and Empire: Religion and Power in Roman Imperial Society*, ed.
Richard A. Horsley, pp. 206–214, (Pennsylvania: Trinity Press International, 1997), p. 209.

A Religio-Political Model of Church in Thessalonica

The first of Paul's letters was written to a small group of house churches in Thessalonica. What do we know of the factors that influenced the ethos and culture of Thessalonica in Paul's time? Thessalonica, a city in Macedonia, was founded by the Greek Empire in 316 BCE. When Macedonia became a Roman province in 146 BCE Thessalonica was named its capital and the centre of Roman administration. This decision was based on its position on a small bay that afforded access to the tributaries of the Danube. Also it boasted an all-weather road that connected the Adriatic to the Aegean. While under Roman rule Macedonia was invaded many times, which left the Macedonians with a 'siege mentality'.[3] 'Peace and Security' was a continuous concern and was maintained by military action. When Paul first arrived in Thessalonica, around 50 CE, it was a cosmopolitan city, boasting a population of around forty thousand people from all around the Mediterranean.[4] Claudius was Roman emperor and Thessalonica was a prosperous, provincial city and had been a loyal Roman colony for two hundred years.

Paul would have witnessed Thessalonian support for the empire everywhere he looked. One building, in particular, would have dominated the landscape, the temple built during Augustus' reign to honour the emperor as *imperator*, 'son of god' and 'god incarnate'.[5] The title *imperator*, meaning 'all-conquering one', was the most important of the three titles and gave meaning to the other two. Augustus was believed to have merited the title 'son of god' on account of his extraordinary prowess as military leader

---

3. Abraham Smith, 'Unmasking the Powers: Towards a Postcolonial Analysis of 1 Thessalonians' in *Paul and the Roman Imperial Order*, ed. by Richard A. Horsley, pp. 47–66 (London: Trinity Press International, 2004), p. 64.

4. John Dominic Crossan and Jonathan L. Reed, *In Search Of Paul: How Jesus's Apostle Opposed Rome's Empire with God's Kingdom* (New York: HarperSanFrancisco, 2004), p. 155.

5. Marcus J. Borg and John Dominic Crossan, *The First Paul: Reclaiming the radical visionary behind the church's conservative icon* (London: SPCK, 2009), pp. 101–104.

and victor. He brought peace and stability to the empire following more than a decade of civil war that had threatened to destroy the Mediterranean world, as well as the empire itself. Further, he achieved divinisation while still alive, and was, therefore, 'god incarnate'. He was believed to be the primary god, among all the gods and goddesses. The Roman poet, Horace, wrote of Augustus:

> Upon you ... while still among us, we already bestow honours, set up altars to swear by in your name, and confess that nothing like you will rise after you or has risen before you.
>
> *(Epistles 21:12–17)*[6]

It was in this theo-political Roman context that Paul preached the gospel of Jesus Christ, as 'the Lord' (1 Thess 1:1) and 'the Son of God', attributing Caesar's divine titles and claims to Christ. This was treasonous and accounts for the Thessalonian reaction to Paul. According to Acts of the Apostles, the house of Paul's sponsor in Thessalonica was attacked and Jason and other members of the house church were dragged before the *ekklesia*, or city authorities, for judgement. The Jews and persons from the marketplace brought the following accusation:

> These men who have turned the world upside down have come here also, and Jason has received them; and they are all acting against the decrees of Caesar saying that there is another king named Jesus.
>
> *(Acts of the Apostles 17:6–7)*

These protestors were not acting maliciously but were compelled by their oath of loyalty to report cases of disloyalty and, where possible, had to physically hunt down and bring offenders before the civil authorities.[7]

We might surmise that Paul had to leave Thessalonica in rather a hurry due to opposition. The references in Paul's letter

---

6. *Ibid.*, p. 103.

7. Karl P. Donfried, 'The Imperial Cults of Thessalonica and Political Conflict in 1 Thessalonians' in *Paul and Empire*, ed. Horsley, pp. 215–223, p. 222. This oath was referred to as the Paphlagonian oath.

to the ongoing suffering of the members of the Thessalonian house churches, probably numbering no more than two dozen Christians, underlined their continuing persecution for their faith.[8] Those who had 'fallen asleep' so soon (1 Thess 4:13) may have been victims of persecution.

In his letter, Paul took another religio-political term, *parousia*, used to refer to the emperor's approach and visitation of a city, and applied it to the coming of 'our Lord Jesus' (1 Thess 2:19, 3:13). The preparations for the emperor's once-in-a-lifetime visit to a Roman colony were extensive. The visit began with a formal greeting of the emperor at the city gates and was followed with civic sacrifice in the emperor's temple, and festivities involving aristocrats and celebrations for all the people. The tombs of the dead were along the main approach into the city and the emperor passed by these first, en route to the city.

Unlike the emperor's *parousia*, which is known and prepared for in advance, Paul informed the Thessalonians that the Lord's coming will be like 'a thief in the night' (1 Thess 5:2, 4). Paul used the term to refer to the 'return' or 'second coming' of Christ, the final eschatological visitation, a one-time visit, like that of the emperor. The *parousia* of Christ will establish God's reign on earth, which began with Jesus' resurrection. Unlike the Roman Empire, which achieved peace through military violence and victory, God's peace would be achieved non-violently by fairness and justice. The Thessalonian Christians were, therefore, to resist the Roman world view and live an alternative Christian life, shielding themselves from attack by wearing the 'breastplate of faith and love, and for a helmet the hope of salvation' (1 Thess 5:8). The 'Day of the Lord' imagery resonated with the apocalyptic language of the exilic prophet Deutero-Isaiah who, in a different imperial context, was also speaking of resistance. Paul's good news for the suffering Thessalonians was that they were not just waiting for 'the day of the Lord' but were actually living it, and

---

8. Paul refers to the opposition he and his co-workers faced when in Thessalonica (1 Thess. 2:2) and to the ongoing persecution of church members, even unto death (1 Thess. 1:6–7, 2:14–15, 3:3).

already belonged to its light (1 Thess 5:5). Paul consoled the suffering community by reminding them to place their hope in God who promised real and everlasting peace, the antithesis of Roman peace, which would not last (1 Thess 5:23).

Paul was asking this minority, suffering church to witness to a religio-political model of church that announced Christ as the true 'Lord' and 'Son of God', and not the emperor. Their suffering, like that of Christ's, exposed the violence of imperial power and their hope in Christ's *parousia* was a reminder to the Thessalonian society that all human empires were transitory and only God's reign would be everlasting. Considering the insignificant size of the Thessalonian church, and the power of empire promoting the imperial cult, this church model was reliant on its membership demonstrating radical and courageous faith. Conscious of this, Paul spoke of his own struggles with empire and reminded the Thessalonian house churches that they would find the strength to resist empire if they remembered the faithfulness of the 'living and true God' (1 Thess 1:9). This model of church challenged all ultimate claims to power, security and peace.

The religio-political model of church in Thessaonica illustrates that while church is political, that is, concerned with justice, compassion and peace for the whole community, this is very different from being 'politicised'. In Northern Ireland, in particular, churches have bought into partisan politics and identified with different sections of the community over against 'the other'. Churches have mirrored the sectarianism in society and given it religious justification. The challenge is to transform church so that all denominations are committed to the common good. The two key questions are: does denominationalism allow for this transformation; and do our churches have a vision for the common good?

An Equality Model of Church in Galatia
As in Thessalonica, the model of church that developed in Galatia addressed particular concerns and witnessed to another way of being community. What do we know of Galatia in the first century CE? Augustus established the Roman province of Galatia from a disparate array of tribes: the Phyrigians, Pisidians and

Celts, to name a few. These groups, who had previously escaped Hellenisation and retained their own languages, customs and religions were, under Roman domination, given a common identity and expected to accept the Roman religion and imperial culture. When Paul arrived in Galatia the province was in the process of becoming a Roman, urban centre.

Acts of the Apostles records Paul visiting Pisidian Antioch twice (13–14). It boasted an imperial temple, which sat on the city's highest point and was visible for miles around. As with other imperial temples it faced Rome, and was dedicated to Caesar Augustus, 'son of god'.[9] In the north of Galatia, citizens had to take an oath promising allegiance to Augustus, which ensured loyalty, whilst promoting collegiality. Breaking the oath was considered an act of treason, punishable by death. Each resident promised:

> I swear by Zeus, the Earth, the Sun, and by all the gods and goddesses, including Augustus himself, to be favourable to Caesar Augustus, his sons and his descendents forever, in speech, in actions, and in thoughts, considering as friends those he considers so, and regarding as enemies those he judges so, and to defend their interests I will spare neither body, nor soul, nor life, nor my children ...[10]

The Galatian church, like the church in Thessalonica, was part of a contrast culture movement that stood in tension with the wider Greco-Roman society. Examination of the letter Paul sent to the house churches in Galatia around 53 CE evidences that while with them he had preached a gospel of inclusivity and equality for all. The opposition Paul had anticipated in Galatia, following his visit, did not in this instance originate from the Romans. The disagreement was an internal one led by the circumcision party.

It seems supporters of circumcision for gentiles had entered Galatia in Paul's wake and told his converts that Paul's teaching

---

9. Crossan and Reed, *In Search Of Paul*, p. 204.
10. *Ibid.*, p. 206.

was askew, that in fact circumcision and adhering to dietary laws were essential criteria for admittance to the Christian faith. Further, that Paul was not even an Apostle, but a subordinate missionary who was in disagreement with his superiors in Jerusalem and Antioch.[11] Their version of the gospel, in contrast to what Paul taught, assumed that people's access to Christ required they obey the Mosaic Law, or at least some of its major requirements.

In his letter Paul affirmed his status as an Apostle sent 'through Jesus Christ and God the Father, who raised him from the dead' (Gal 1:1). He further confirmed that the gospel he received did not come from human origin but was the result of a divine call at Damascus (Gal 1:11–13). Paul argued, as he had done at the Jerusalem Council and later Antioch, that because gentiles had already received the Spirit of God, prior to either circumcision or adherence to dietary laws, these traditions could not be imposed on them.

It appears the circumcision party had justified the need for circumcision as a sign of covenant with reference to Genesis 17, God's covenant with Abraham. John Dominic Crossan and Jonathan Reed believe that they likely 'emphasised that all of Abraham's male progeny were circumcised, whether slave-born through Hagar and Ishmael, or free-born through Sarah and Isaac.'[12] On the basis of this the circumcision party may have concluded that all descendents of Hagar and Sarah, whether Arab or Jew, must observe the full Torah and be circumcised.

In his counter-argument Paul drew on an earlier covenant tradition from Genesis 15, which made the point that God entered

---

11. *Ibid.*, p. 200. Some scholars believe that on his return to Galatia, after he and Barnabas split at Syrian Antioch following the difference of opinion over eating with the uncircumcised, Paul focused his efforts in Northern Galatia. Barnabas had guardianship of the Christian assemblies in the southern part of Galatia. But the issue that had initially united Paul and Barnabas, their opposition to the circumcision of gentile Christians, and later divided them when Barnabas sided with Peter who favoured circumcision for gentiles, was far from resolved. This incident is recorded in Galatians 2:11–14.
12. Crossan and Reed, *In Search Of Paul*, p. 224.

into covenant with Abraham because of the latter's faith. Therefore, Paul argued, faith not circumcision was what counted. Further, the blessings promised to Abraham were available to gentiles redeemed by their faith in the crucified Christ 'from the curse of the law', which had condemned Christ (Gal 3:13–14).

It is worth remembering at this point that circumcision was not only a means of distinguishing Jew from gentile, it was also a wholly male ritual, incorporating the male child, or adult in the case of converts, into the community of the law; and, according to Genesis 17:13, 'Both the slave born in your house and the one bought with your money must be circumcised.' There is, consequently, a triple distinction and triple hierarchy underpinning Paul's opponents' understanding of circumcision as outlined in Genesis 17:9–14.[13]

At about the time Paul's letter was written, another rite was coming into favour for initiation of converts, ritual immersion or baptism for both sexes. It is thought that behind Paul's words in Galatians 3:27–28 was a baptismal ritual of the early church.

> As many of you as were baptised into Christ have clothed yourself with Christ. There is no longer Jew or Greek, there is no longer slave or free, there is no longer male or female, for all of you are one in Christ Jesus.

Baptism into Christ eradicated all the major divisions separating people: racial, class and gender. It created a new people, where all prior given or chosen identity-definitions were transcended. This new creation, or new humanity, was not to be understood individualistically as a person receiving a new 'nature' or new 'self' in Christ. This is a post-Enlightenment view. Rather, in Christ a whole new social reality was brought into being in which dividing walls were broken down, former enemies reconciled, and God created a new people. Baptism, then as now, was understood as the sacrament of radical equality, breaking down barriers between people. Paul, in his letter, reminded the Galatian house churches that their mission was to celebrate this truth about baptism by treating each other as equals.

---

13. *Ibid.*, p. 227.

What is obvious from this letter is that for Paul the principle of equality challenges the foundations of the Greco-Roman world view, which relied on patriarchy and slavery as a foundation for ordering society around households. The *pater familias*, the male head of the household, was in charge, and the emperor was viewed as the ultimate patriarch to whom all were answerable. The patronage system relied on a hierarchical society with slaves on the bottom rung. It maintained the status quo and managed class conflict by holding out the possibility that faithful service might result in manumission and freedom to move upwards.

In Paul's view all baptised were equal because they were one in Christ. Paul challenged the church at Galatia to reject all inequalities as 'Christian gender inequality can no more exist than can Christian class inequality'.[14] Paul's letter to Philemon underlines how he regarded the idea that a Christian should own a slave as an oxymoron. Regarding females and males in the Christian community, Paul held they were to be equal in family, assembly and apostolate.

Schussler Fiorenza points out that this equality status would have caused particular problems for men within the Christian community and larger Greco-Roman society:

> Just as born Jews had to abandon the privileged notion that they alone were the chosen people of God, so masters had to relinquish their power over slaves, and husbands that over wives and children. The legal-societal and cultural-religious male privileges were no longer valid for Christians.[15]

Difficulties would have arisen for women and slaves who became Christian while remaining in pagan marriages and households. Their alternative vision and praxis would have clashed with the dominant household code.

---

14. *Ibid.*, p. 110.
15. Elisabeth Schussler Fiorenza, 'The Praxis of Coequal Discipleship' in *Paul and Empire*, ed. Horsley, pp. 224–241, p. 230.

The radical nature of the equality vision Paul held up for the Galatian house churches might have appealed to those suppressed by society's norms, as it offered greater freedom. But likely those used to status in the wider community would have struggled with loss of privileges. Living an equality model of church, in opposition to the surrounding community, was certainly not an easy option and would have created tensions within the house churches and most certainly in the wider community. Yet it was the only option. Paul knew from experience that divisions based on class, ethnicity and gender destroy community. Following Jesus, he advocated an inclusive egalitarian community model. This way of being church and community challenged the basis of Greco-Roman society, providing an alternative. Where there are inequalities, divisions and injustices, this model of church will continue to offer that counter-cultural vision and praxis. Paul returns to this theme of inclusivity in his letter to the Corinthians.

The equality model of church in Galatia stood in opposition to sectarianism, racism, sexism and classism, which construes difference as inequality and justifies difference of treatment on the grounds of status and subordination. The key issue for Paul was 'Who is being excluded and on what grounds?' As part of the Belfast Agreement, Section 75 of the 1998 Government of Northern Ireland Act was introduced to ensure that equality of opportunity and good relations would be central to public policy making. The nine categories of people listed in Section 75 are: those of different religious belief, political opinion, racial group, age, marital status, sexual orientation, men and women generally, persons with a disability and persons without, and persons with dependents and persons without. It is illegal for public authorities to discriminate against any of these categories of people. Though churches are not considered to be public authorities they are moral communities and as such have a moral obligation to affirm the equality of all categories. The Pauline vision of the church in Galatians is of a radically inclusive community that anticipates the ethos and emphases of Section 75. The challenge faced by the Galatian church, to practise a truly inclusive model of church, remains a challenge for Irish churches today.

A Just Economic Model of Church in Corinth

The model of church Paul called for in Corinth was again a response to the needs of the community. What do we know about the development of Corinth as a Roman colony? In 146 BCE Rome forced a war with Corinth, then ruthlessly sacked the city, killing a majority of its men and enslaving its women and children. In 44 BCE Julius Caesar refounded Corinth making it a Roman colony and filling the place with army veterans and large numbers of urban poor from Rome, over half of whom were freed slaves.[16] The community in Corinth were consequently comprised of 'haves' and 'have-nots'. Handsomely built houses dwarfed poorer residences. Rich and poor lived uncomfortably side by side; the latter's misery all the more obvious when compared to the extreme wealth of the former. The ruling body, the *Polis*, represented those with honour, power and wealth who supported the cult of the emperor and other religious cults.

When Paul visited Corinth we are told he formed a friendship with Prisca and her husband Aquila who became his co-workers (Acts 18:2–3). With their assistance he met with small groups in people's houses (1 Cor 16:19), choosing to avoid the marketplace where different religious groups vied for primacy (2 Cor 2:17).

We learn from Paul's two extant letters to the Corinthian house churches that they mirrored the same deep socio-economic divisions in the wider society. Church membership included people from diverse ethnic origins and different social strata. The Corinthian church was in fact a microcosm of Corinthian society. The majority of members were drawn from the lower socio-economic strata of Corinthian society, so wealthy members were in the minority. Paul drew attention to this fact: 'Consider your own call, brothers and sisters: not many of you were wise by human standards, not many were powerful, not many were of noble birth' (1 Cor 1:26).

There were also theological and cultural divisions in the house churches. Some supported Paul, others Apollos, others Cephas,

---

16. Richard A. Horsley, '1 Corinthians: A Case Study of Paul's Assembly as an Alternative Society' in *Paul and Empire*, ed. Horsley, pp. 242–252, pp. 242–3.

and others were of the Christ party. In his correspondence Paul
challenged this division. He worried that on his initial visit to the
city he might have unwittingly sowed the seeds of misunder-
standing. On that occasion he had singled out influential individuals in Corinth for baptism, which may have suggested to them
a patronal relationship of sorts.[17] It seems one or other of the
Corinthian householders, who allowed their spacious homes to
be used for church meetings, worship and Eucharist, and who
had the financial where-with-all to contribute to Paul and other
Apostles' support, hoped to enhance their own prestige in the
church by serving as a patron. Although Paul accepted financial
support from other churches, he expressly refused to do so from
the Corinthians (1 Cor 9:11–15). In light of the prevailing misun-
derstanding Paul was determined to underline the difference between the Christian community, which was based on practising
economic equality and the patronal Roman community, which
was premised on inequality.

Paul emphasised, in his letters, that social relations have an
economic basis; therefore Corinthian Christians must develop an
alternative to the hierarchical, socio-economic patronage system.
Paul understood how economics underpinned the social and civil
institutions. He, therefore, suggested the Corinthians follow an
alternative egalitarian economic system. He knew that practising
a just economic system would mean creating alternative structures within the Christian community.

Instead of the vertical tributary system that operated in the
Greco-Roman world, which ensured money flowed from the subjects back to the emperor, Paul advanced a horizontal economic
system between the churches. He organised and administered a
collection for the poor in Jerusalem and asked the Corinthians to
give financial aid (1 Cor 16:1–4). Paul may have drawn his
inspiration from the Mosaic covenantal ideal, which upheld the
principle that each community member should have enough to
live on (Lev 25).

---

17. 1 Corinthians 1:14–16 mentions that Paul baptised Crispus, who was
'official of the synagogue', (Acts of the Apostles 18:8); Gaius, 'host to me
and to the whole church', (Romans 16:23); and the household of
Stephanus.

Paul was aware of the corruption of the justice system, which favoured the powerful and those who could afford bribes. He insisted financial disputes be settled inside the community rather than in the civil courts (1 Cor 6:1–8). Public festivals were particularly important occasions, as they provided a forum for elites to make important contacts that would lead to lucrative economic ventures. However, attendance of elites from the house churches at city banquets in pagan temples was creating difficulties in the Christian community, as the meat eaten at these banquets was first offered in sacrifice to the temple gods. Paul warned against participation at religious festivals and sharing in food offered to idols (1 Cor 10:14–21).

For Paul the eucharistic meal was the Christian model of social and economic cohesion. It was a radical alternative to the Greco-Roman festivals, for it expressed an inclusivity and cohesion that exposed the injustice at the heart of the patronage system. In Paul's opinion, slaves and nobodies were on an equal footing with the elite at the eucharistic celebration – all were members of the same body. The radical equality of all who shared Eucharist in the house churches was, however, being overlooked in Corinth.

First-century Christian eucharistic sharing took place in the context of a full meal. Community members were to bring what food they had and share it with others, recalling the hospitality of the shared-meals Jesus participated in as part of his ministry. This share-meal also symbolised the Jewish covenantal idea that the world was God's and humans were but stewards participating in the fruits of God's creation. For the early church the sacrament of Eucharist was meant to bring about the communion of those gathered around each table, as well as the communion of all local churches.

However, when the Corinthian Christians met to celebrate the Eucharist the deep economic divisions became evident. The elite arrived first, as they had plenty of leisure time, unlike the poor who had work commitments. The wealthy brought along expensive cuts of meat, and instead of sharing these with the poor, ate the portions themselves. Seating arrangements also tended to follow the custom established in the Greco-Roman society, with the most important person seated in the best seat, flanked on either side by those next in line. When the slaves arrived there was little left to eat and so they were deprived of what should have been a decent meal (1 Cor 11:21). The Eucharist at Corinth had become an expression of division and the division was economic.

Angered at the actions of the elite, Paul wrote, 'Do you show contempt for the church of God and humiliate those who have nothing?' (1 Cor 11:22) He used the 'body' metaphor, an established political metaphor in Corinth, where it referred to the citizen body of the city state, to drive home his point. The Corinthian house churches were to model God's design for the whole 'body politic'. They were to be a distinctive faith community in the public square of Corinthian life. 'There are many members, yet one body', Paul insisted (1 Cor 12:20). As the one body of Christ they had responsibility for each other. He called on the Corinthian house churches to become a community of interdependence, where everyone was equal and recognised their need of each others' gifts. Further, as a Christian body they were to remember that they belonged to Christ and shared, with Christ, God's Spirit (1 Cor 12:12–13). Equality in community for Paul was about parity based on members having diverse gifts and experiences that enhanced the community. It was not about sameness or uniformity but difference, inclusivity, and partnership rooted in the different gifts of the Spirit.

The church in Corinth, then, was to model a healthy citizen body and a measure of its robustness was the well-being of each of its members. Unity within the church and between its members was premised on just economic sharing and practices. Eucharistic sharing without economic sharing and inclusivity missed the point. Such unity both preceded eucharistic sharing and was affirmed in the sacramental encounter. This model of church challenges all forms of church to reconsider their theology and praxis of Eucharist and economics.

The just economic church in Corinth, with its concern to be in solidarity with the poor, provided an alternative ethos and praxis to the Greco-Roman patronage system. Paul reminded the Corinthians that economic sharing within the community of faith, which arose from the desire to offer mutual support to each other, was at the core of what it meant to be the body of Christ. And that excluding the poor, or leaving their situation unchanged, while participating in Eucharist, was to invite judgement (1 Cor 11:29). Economic sharing in the name of Jesus is at the heart of eucharistic sharing. Participation in the Eucharist unites us with Christ in his self-gift to God. We affirm and are strengthened in our commitment to follow Christ in his liberation of all that oppresses and divides. In our day, as in Paul's, economics is still the primary source of much division. Paul challenged the Corinthians to consider their poor and contribute to the well-being of the poor in other places, like Jerusalem by sending financial support. How can the churches in Ireland gauge whether they are responding to the challenge of Eucharist in both local and international contexts?

There are a number of questions that might be asked to elicit information on what the churches are, or are not, doing in pursuit of economic justice. Who are the poor in our midst and how is the church to be involved alongside the poor? How aware are those who make decisions and influence thinking within the church of social policies that disadvantage the poor? Is the church involved in mobilising for change to such policies, by lobbying politicians or educating the membership? Or is the church a middle-class institution colluding with society to keep the poor in poverty by maintaining the status quo?

The Eucharist as a practice also challenges worldly economic and social structures that benefit those living in the Northern hemisphere. It is hard to comprehend that in the poorest of countries a child dies every few seconds from hunger. The connection of the Eucharist with the hungry of the world and those who have no bread cannot be ignored. On a global scale how are the churches responding to hunger, division and injustice? How can the eucharistic feast, like the multiplication of loaves and fishes, become a living symbol of the openness and generosity of the Christian community? Is the church's ultimate loyalty to the reign of God or the reign of the market?

And sharing Eucharist was also an inclusive experience, uniting the community with Christ. Participation in Eucharist, where there was no unity of relationships, was frowned upon by Paul. Does this perspective challenge Irish churches to reconsider the importance of relational unity as a pre-requisite for participation in Eucharist? In other words, where there is relational disunity among Christians should there be the celebration of Eucharist?[18]

A Kenotic Model of Power in Phillippi

Paul also corresponded with the Christian house churches in Philippi, another loyal colony of the Roman Empire. In Philippi public life was meant to mirror life in the empire and Philippian citizens were expected, in their civic life, to demonstrate their allegiance to Rome. As in other Roman colonies, the practice of patronage operated here and embedded inequalities into the social system, serving to distribute power from the top down. This caused rivalry and factionalism within the city. In the public arena, and in the civil courts, individuals were treated according to prestige and social standing. This competition for promotion and power impacted the churches Paul corresponded with.

The Christian community in Philippi were viewed with suspicion and considered 'unworthy' citizens of Rome by other Philippian citizens. This was because of their withdrawal from participation in the city's cult practices and their rejection of patronage. Living, as they did, in the centre of Philippian society, they were, however, influenced by the power struggles and partisan behaviour of public life. Consequently disputes over power and control, similar to those in the surrounding society, also arose within the Christian community. These disputes threatened the unity and ethos of the church.

Paul, aware of the situation, wrote his letter to the Philippian house churches to address this power-struggle within the church. The original church at Philippi was of gentile origin and began in Lydia's house. Women continued in leadership positions within the Philippian house churches and two in particular,

---

18. Paul is not insisting on theological unity or doctrinal unity. Such unity has never existed, not even in churches of the Christian Testament. Theological unity only became a concern in the 9th century CE. Given the history of the church from the beginning this was a misguided concern.

Euodia and Syntyche, were involved in a very serious power struggle, which was creating factions within the churches, leading to division. Paul feared that the private dispute could become so serious it might be perceived as undermining public order by the Philippian authorities and be referred to the law and civil courts, thus discrediting the gospel.

In his letter, he sought to encourage the Philippian Christians to live as 'citizens worthy of the gospel of Christ'. He reminded them that they were to be of 'the same mind'. His appeal for harmony and concord, mutual regard and affection within the *ekklesia* was deliberately opposed to the values of rivalry that permeated the surrounding culture. Paul reminded them that their life on earth was to be governed by the heavenly commonwealth, and that their lives should therefore reflect God's laws and values, rather than those of the Roman Empire.

Paul recognised that the house churches were in a prime position to influence for good the surrounding community. He expressed a hope that their efforts to publicly model a more participatory form of community might impact power relations within the life of the city. It was in this context, then, that they were to live 'as citizens worthy of the gospel'.

Paul cited the Christological hymn, which recounts Christ's choice to give up equality with God in order to become a slave (Phil 2:6–11). He reminds the Philippians that Christ did not cease to be in the form of God when he took the form of a slave, anymore than he ceased to be the Son of God when he became man. Rather, it was in his self-emptying that Jesus revealed what God is like. In his taking the form of a slave we see something of God. This is not a God of almighty power, reflected in the image of the Roman emperor. This was no Caesar who expected piety from his followers and who maintained his power through war, establishing peace through victory. There was no absolutist, dominating, or coercive use of power here.

Paul argued that Jesus did not grasp at primacy, that is his equal status with God, and as a result Christ had been given a primacy of servanthood, which all creation would acknowledge. Instead of grasping at dominance, Paul challenged the Philippian

Christians to empty themselves of dominating power and privileged status. This was a model of power that served rather than dominated. Paul was suggesting it was a model of power for the public place.

Paul drew on first-century Philippian political vocabulary to compare the power displayed by the Roman Empire with the model of power he recommended for the Christian community. The empire's power was marked by 'unworthy' behaviour, namely, discord, strife, partisan activity, competitive party spirit, intense hatred and the need for primacy. The model Paul recommended by contrast was one that was worthy of followers of Christ. The values at the heart of this model of power were concord, harmony in public life, politics of friendship, freedom, political health and unity.

At the heart of Paul's message to the Philippians is the notion that Christians should be prepared to be radically vulnerable for the sake of Christ, as the cross is the foundation of the Christian community. The nature of the community and the social ethos Paul advocated is a direct challenge to the abuse of power and state control that operated in the Roman Empire.

The kenotic model of power Paul outlines in his letter to the Philippians raises questions about the nature of power and how it is organised and distributed within church structures. Power is relational, everyone has it. Power is an energy, which allows us to accomplish something. We cannot see power, only its effect. There is no one way for power to function; it can flow top down, bottom up, or be shared. Authority is legitimated power. The basis for authority in human relations is the need for guidance. We need the security of others' guidance. Those who attribute authority to a minister and scripture do so because they believe God speaks to them through both. When we begin to question some forms of authority we look for other forms of legitimate authority for guidance. In religion, authority is the most powerful form of power because it functions not by forcing people but by giving them assurance. Religion functions by legitimated power. While authority can be understood as legitimated power, like other forms of power, authority can be corrupted. Authority can be used in illegitimate ways to manipulate or destroy. An audit determining how power is exercised in church can be helpful in exposing the system of power operating and its impact.[19]

Power that is abusive, exploitative, oppressive, dehumanising or elitist contradicts the kenotic power Christ modelled. Kenotic power is about service given from abundance of love not scarcity. It is a different model of power, and exposes 'power over', or 'power as domination', or 'power as privilege and status' models as oppressive and exploitative. Jesus, in his own life, showed that leadership is about empowering others, ensuring all are included. Jesus' leadership, ultimately, was cruciform, and involved suffering love. It is suffering in the face of opposition to empire and the authority that empire represented. His sacrifice can be reinterpreted as liberation, which is the root of the word salvation.[20] Furthermore, the Christological hymn in Philippians emphasises that power as love is the very nature of the Triune God. The kenotic love that flows between the persons of the Trinity is one of mutual giving and receiving. The whole church is called to live out of this kenotic model of power that in the end is life-affirming, for it is rooted in advocacy and the struggle in community for justice and empowerment of the marginalised.

What challenge does this present for Irish churches? It means the churches need to be involved in owning their own abuses of power. In the instance of clerical abuses and 'cover-up', those with responsibility to serve within the church need to engage with victims and survivors of abuse to fully embrace their

---

19. The following questions might be included in a questionnaire auditing power: In church what is happening beneath the surface? Where is the intellectual power? Who tells people what truth is? How is power mediated – by a dominant person or a group? How does the class system operate? How do groups within the church relate? Where is the economic power? How is it managed? Who holds political power? And who is involved in decision making?

20. Salvation is liberation in lived experience. Church is present wherever God's will is being done, wherever justice and peace are being pursued, wherever the poor and marginalised are experiencing justice and liberation from oppression, whatever form it takes.

failings, lament their failure and learn how to become advocates for radical justice. This has already begun in a number of dioceses in Ireland. 'Putting on the mind of Christ' also challenges all within the churches to rid themselves of sectarianism, racism, classism and patriarchy. For each of these hierarchical systems is an abuse of power, divisive of relationships and contrary to the 'mind of Christ'.

Church as Sign of the Kingdom of God in Matthew
Matthew's gospel is unique among the four in its use of the word *ekklesia* and consequently is often viewed as the 'gospel of the church'. For Matthew *ekklesia* was a gathered people whose roots and practice were in the Jewish tradition. Matthew's Jewish understanding of *ekklesia* was of a gathered people who shared Jesus' ethical commitment to fulfill the Jewish Law and prophets, by realising God's alternative kingdom. According to Matthew, the authority Jesus taught with, and acted from, was rooted in the authority of God and based on justice, mercy, compassion and peace, the core covenant values. Matthew's gospel is also the only one where the word *matheteutheis* appears, which translates as 'one learned' in the teacher's ways, or 'one discipled' to a teacher who practices what she/he has been taught.[21] *Ekklesia*, for Matthew then, was a house church where members were educated in the way of discipleship, where all were under God's reign, and discipled in the ethos and vision of God's kingdom.

For Matthew *ekklesia* was counter-cultural, an alternative to the Roman imperial household system. For this reason Matthew highlighted how Jesus' call to discipleship, to be 'fishers of people' (Mt 4:19), was an invitation to join Jesus in his struggle to overturn the existing order of power and privilege. The fishing image has its roots in Jeremiah, Amos and Ezekiel, who used it to denounce the elites' false worship (Jer 16:16), as a euphemism for an unjust lifestyle of 'oppressing the poor and crushing the

---

21. Michael H. Crosby, 'Matthew's Gospel: The Disciples' Call to Justice' in *The New Testament: Introducing the Way of Discipleship*, eds. Wess Howard-Brook and Sharon H. Ringe, pp. 16–39 (New York: Orbis Books, 2002), p. 17.

needy' (Amos 4:2), and as a judgement on imperial power (Ezek 29:3). Commitment to Jesus, Matthew indicated, took precedence over all other allegiances and belonging to God's kingdom entailed challenging oppressive and dominating imperial powers. The disciples' mission, and in turn the mission of the *ekklesia*, was to proclaim and make real God's empire (Mt 10:7–8).

Matthew is also the only gospel writer to use the term 'kingdom of heaven' interchangeably with 'kingdom of God'. He does not differentiate between the two terms as 'heaven' is a euphemism for God. For Matthew this kingdom was a place of healing, holiness, wholeness and shalom, in other words a place of salvation. Matthew's Beatitudes, which begin the Sermon on the Mount, were written for those who believed God's liberating dream for the whole of creation had already begun with Jesus. But how were beatitudes understood in Matthew's Jewish world?

According to Warren Carter, 'In apocalyptic works beatitudes declare God's future transformation or reversal of present dismal circumstances.'[22] Matthew divided his Beatitudes (Mt 5:3–12) into two sections. The first four focused on oppressive situations reversed in God's kingdom. 'The poor in spirit' were those crushed by economic injustice, yet they are exhorted to hope that God's salvation will come. 'Those who mourn' were weeping at the destructive nature of imperial power, which destroys life. However, they will be comforted when God ends oppression and establishes God's justice. 'The meek', who trusted in God's promise to overthrow the oppressor and did not seek opportunities to exact revenge, would 'inherit the earth'. This is an affirmation that the land and its resources belonged to God and in God's kingdom all would have access. Those who 'hunger and thirst' because of unjust imperial practices would under God's reign experience just societal relationships. Righteousness, Matthew reminded his church, encompassed personal integrity, social justice and a commitment to peace building.

The remaining four Beatitudes outline human actions considered honourable under God's reign. The 'merciful' forgive even

22. Warren Carter, *Matthew and the Margins: A Sociopolitical and Religious Reading* (New York: Orbis Books, 2000), p. 130.

enemies and treat all with respect and love, a practice at odds with the Jewish world view. The 'pure in heart', living according to God's kingdom values, would one day see God. 'Peacemakers' who non-violently resisted Roman military might and cultural domination, seeking the well-being of all, were living as God would wish them. Finally, those 'persecuted' by empire for challenging the status quo and seeking justice and equitable distribution of resources, were participating in, and would one day enjoy, the fullness of God's empire. In Matthew the stress is on realising a just and healthy society.[23]

Jesus' third discourse begins in chapter 13 in Matthew. The previous two, (chapters 5–7, 10), outlined the negative response Jesus and his teaching would receive from those with vested interests in imperial power. Jesus, in a series of parables on the kingdom of God, explained the lack of receptivity to his kingdom message. In the parable of the tares and wheat (Mt 13:24–30) Jesus is speaking out of an Eastern context, where wheat and weeds grow together and are indistinguishable until the moment of harvest. The parable takes seriously that the *ekklesia* was both theological community formed by God's grace and sociological community that was flawed, where members find themselves colluding with, or mirroring, the world values at odds with those of God's kingdom. The *ekklesia* is never pure wheat but always in need of transformation.

Matthew 26:6–13 illustrates the faithfulness required from a disciple when opposed by those who wish to deny God's reign. The incident describes the anointing of Jesus' head with costly ointment by an unnamed woman. The anointing had a triple function, which was understood by Jesus but missed by the disciples who were more concerned with the apparent waste of money. Her action was a profound act of hospitality, an anticipation of Jesus' death and burial and a sign that Jesus was the 'Anointed One' or 'Messiah'. Like the prophets in the Hebrew Scriptures who anointed future kings, her gesture is prophetic. She recognised God's kingdom was diametrically opposed to the Roman Empire, which would crush him to protect itself. She also

23. *Ibid.*, pp.131–137.

realised that suffering and death awaited those who followed Jesus, and who resisted the empire's ideology and practices. For Matthew she is an example of a true disciple.

The final scene in this gospel is a commissioning story (Mt 28: 16–20). Although the narrative mentions the 'eleven', it is likely there were women present as well. Matthew has already indicated that at the cross 'Many women were also there, looking on from a distance; they had followed Jesus from Galilee and they provided for him' (Mt 27:55). Matthew identified them as true disciples through the use of the formula: they 'followed Jesus' (Mt 4:20–22). He further indicated that the women were charged by an angel, and the risen Jesus, to tell the disciples to go to Galilee. The choice of place was significant for Matthew. Galilee was at the periphery, on the margins of Israel, and those living in Galilee were despised and considered unclean by the religious leaders in Jerusalem. Matthew was challenging those who considered themselves to be at the centre of religious and social status.

The key words of the commission are to 'make disciples', sharing faith by word and action, and to 'teach'. Jesus was sending his disciples out into the whole world, to Jews and gentiles, to translate his teachings and initiate disciples into the new community, the *ekklesia*, through baptism. Baptism was initiation into God's alternative empire of social justice and peace. Matthew used this commissioning scene to define the mission of the church as disciple-making. For Matthew, missionary discipleship was about belonging to a community where eyes and ears were open to recognise injustice, suffering and oppression. It was also about belonging to a community of action where people together practised God's social justice to the poor, marginalised and excluded. Discipleship was committed action for God's alternative empire in which justice, right relations and peacemaking were primary. His last scene, consequently, looks forward to God's future reign and an end to all oppression, whatever its source.

A key insight in Matthew, pertinent for Irish churches in the present climate, is the awareness of the fallibility of any model of church. In history the church can never be anything other than a mix of wheat and tares, as such church will always be wholly inadequate. This is a reminder to all of the churches, whatever the particular model, that there is no pure, true church. What is required of church is humility, and the foresight that no church is in a position to make moralistic claims for itself. Further, when a particular model of church becomes oppressive then judgement occurs in history. Times of crisis, or judgement, are also opportunities for purification and transformation, as we await the establishment of God's reign in all its fullness. To mission effectively in the interim period, churches have a responsibility to adhere to the core teachings, values and activities of God's kingdom.

For Matthew the model of church that best equipped his community to be a sign of the kingdom of God was one committed to lifelong learning in the way of discipleship. The core kingdom/ covenant values at the heart of his church were mercy, justice, truth and peace. It was a mission church concerned to witness to and bring these values to the world. In the sectarian context that is Northern Ireland there is a particular onus on churches to learn together how best to respond to this shared Christian mission. The challenge for the Catholic Church, at the present time, is to move beyond institutionalism and, with the help of the wider community, recover the centrality of the kingdom values. The challenge for those Protestant churches who have interpreted mission as evangelism is to recognise that the Spirit of God is at work in all spheres of life, and God's kingdom is broader than any church and includes 'all things in heaven and earth' (Eph 1:10).

These Christian Testament models of church offer churches in Northern Ireland fresh insights into what it means to be church in this twenty-first-century context. One thing that stands out is the 'kingdom consciousness' shared by all the churches explored.

> Kingdom consciousness means living and working in the firm hope of the final triumph of God's reign. In the face of contrary evidence, kingdom Christians hold on to the conviction that God will eventually swallow up all evil, hate and injustice.[24]

24. John Fuellenbach, *The Kingdom of God: The Message of Jesus Today* (New York: Orbis Books, 1995), p. 272.

Fuellenbach underlines the necessity for churches in the twenty-first century to recover the 'transcendent horizon' contained in the kingdom of God symbol. He sees it as an antidote to the temptation to become inward looking, or caught in maintaining systems and structures. The symbol is also a sign of contradiction for churches obsessed with institutional power and control of the faith community. The kingdom of God is always larger than the church. And as Matthew's gospel reminds us, the kingdom of God is to be found in all the world, especially among the suffering, excluded and discriminated. So it would seem that 'kingdom consciousness' is an essential mindset for any church claiming to be Christian.

Whichever models the churches adopt, and there is a plethora in the Christian Testament to choose from, the kingdom vision of Jesus needs to be the horizon informing faith and action. And as the Christian church is impacted by the failure and infidelity of its members, who are always in need of God's mercy and forgiveness, the models it operates from will always stand in need of reform and renewal. According to Matthew, to follow Jesus in the proclamation and living out of God's empire means embracing 'itinerancy, poverty, defencelessness and love'.[25] How willing are the churches to follow this route? What would they need to let go of in order to do so? And how might they travel: in humility engaging God's Spirit within the church and in the wider community; or in isolation convinced those in leadership know the way forward and hoping 'the faithful' will follow?

Having considered our Christian origins let us, in the next chapter, rediscover our Celtic roots and the challenges Celtic monasticism presents to Irish churches.

---

25. Carter, *Matthew and the Margins*, p. 237.

Questions for reflection:

1. What model of church would best meet the need of the local context?

2. The mission of church is to assist in the creation of a just and healthy society that reflects Jesus' kingdom vision. How might the churches in Northern Ireland meet this challenge?

3. Reconciliation is central to any renewal of church, reconciliation within the congregation, with those on the margins or outside, and with those in other denominations. How might the churches in Northern Ireland become places of reconciliation?

Looking Forward to our Celtic Roots

Churches in Ireland have been hidebound by structures and theologies that are territorial, hierarchical, and patriarchal. These systems of relating have their roots in the Christendom model of church. Civil society in Ireland is trying to finds ways out of the violence, economic collapse, and religious quagmire. Territorialism has supported sectarian attitudes, behaviours, and a 'god on our side' theology. Hierarchical systems, whether economic, political, or ecclesial, have failed the people of Ireland. And patriarchy has been oppressive of women and men, damaging relationships, and endorsing inequalities and unethical practices. Churches, as part of civil society, have also to reinvent themselves if they hope to fulfil their ecclesial purpose of witnessing to and teaching the kingdom ethos and values. The Celtic monastic way of being church is one worth reflecting on – not for the purpose of replication. However, the community emphasis, relational values and egalitarian praxis are worthy of recovery. Remembering the past attentively and ethically can help us revision a different future.

The Spread of Monasticism in Ireland

Liam De Paor believed that Christian communities existed from the beginning of the fifth century CE in Ireland, and were made up of Christian slaves, most of whom were British, forcibly brought to Ireland when their Roman provinces were plundered.[1] The system initially adopted from the Western church was one whereby bishops ruled over dioceses with clearly defined boundaries. From mid-fifth century to early sixth century CE the Irish church system, like the political system, underwent huge change, ending with the establishment of monasticism.

---

1. Liam De Paor, *St Patrick's World: The Christian Culture of Ireland's Apostolic Age* (Dublin: Four Courts Press Ltd, 1993), p. 35.

The political structures to which the fifth-century church organisation had initially accommodated were utterly transformed within a few generations, as the political map of Ireland was fundamentally redrawn. And the great organised European system from which Christianity had come to Ireland collapsed within the first generation or so of the effort.[2]

The earliest monastic community in Ireland is thought to have been founded at Kildare around 500 CE by Brigid. As there is no evidence of a male monastery before 535–540 CE it seems likely that women pioneered the monastic movement, which existed until the twelfth century CE in Ireland.[3] These early monasteries were situated in border areas, on previously unsettled land, and they linked the provinces in Ireland. By the eighth century CE Christian monasteries were firmly in existence throughout Ireland, and were established as the primary church structure.[4] The monastic system adopted the tribal and kinship model of Irish society and just as smaller kingdoms looked to the king of kings for protection, and paid tribute accordingly, the most important monastic houses were linked to lesser houses in a confederation (*paruchiae*). The *paruchiae*, under the control of the abbess/abbot, were not limited to former diocesan boundaries. While bishops in Ireland retained their ecclesiastical status and sacramental roles, the abbot/abbess of the mother church, of which Kildare was one, retained administrative power and jurisdiction of the daughter-houses in Ireland and beyond.

> The old bishopric was limited in a narrow territorial area, coextensive with the *plebs* or *tuáth* ('petty kingdom'); the monastic *paruchiae*, on the other hand, could keep on growing and their steady accumulation of lands and property

---

2. *Ibid.*, p. 45.

3. *Ibid.*, p. 49.

4. Michael Richter, *Medieval Ireland: The Enduring Tradition* (Dublin: Gill & Macmillan Ltd, 1988), p. 51.

beyond the boundaries of the *tuáth* meant that the only limit on their growth was the generosity of their benefactors.[5]

The abbess/abbot, in a manner similar to the heads of large kin groups, had responsibility for the members of their community. They had to ensure their legal rights were protected and their physical needs met. As such the abbess/abbot monitored the means of production, controlled the finances, dealt with visitors, regulated the daily rituals, conducted lessons, and made decisions regarding treatment of offenders.[6] Ó Cróinín, referring to a secular law tract (*Córus Béscnai*), which is concerned with the succession to the office of abbess/abbot, indicates that the person designated was chosen from the kin group of the founding saint or, if no candidate was deemed suitable, from the kin group of the person who donated the site for the monastery. Consequently, 'the saint's genealogy constituted a statement of title'.[7] This model of kinship in monastic communities allowed for the retention of property, responsibility and knowledge within the wider family, and ensured family loyalty to monastic communities; it also provided a ready pool of people who could further their careers by replacing those who died.[8]

Political and religious authorities collaborated to maintain peaceful governance of the people. With the assistance of abbesses and abbots, kings could extend their power beyond their *tuáth* boundaries to persuade neighbours and allies to mediate disputes and broker peace treaties. The monastic communities, in turn, ensured that the rights of all people were addressed and that those who were powerless were included in the peace process.[9] The position of monasteries in border areas between

5. Daíbhí Ó Cróinín, *Early Medieval Ireland 400–1200* (London: Longman Group Ltd, 1995), pp. 164–5.
6. Lisa M. Bitel, *Isle of the Saints: Monastic Settlement and Christian Community in Early Ireland* (Cork: Cork University Press, 1990), pp. 89–90.
7. Ó Cróinín, *Early Medieval Ireland*, p. 163.
8. Bitel, *Isles of Saints*, pp. 105–6.
9. *Ibid.*, p. 147.

provinces placed them in a particularly significant location to offer safe space for the settlement of disputes.[10] Monastic communities, from the sixth to the twelfth centuries in Ireland, played a central role in the governance, education and bodily and spiritual development of the Irish people.

Developing a Community Model
In the century or so that followed Patrick's activity in the northern half of Ireland, the church developed a distinctive form. It was not the episcopal model that developed elsewhere in Europe and which, in many ways, mirrored the Roman political administrative system, with dioceses replicating the administrative structures. Perhaps because the Roman imperial system and structures never reached Ireland, the church was always going to reflect a different and more indigenous model.

That said, in the Christendom model the church was one, as was truth. It would be totally misleading to suggest that by the fifth and sixth centuries Ireland was somehow outside Christendom. Following the Edict of Milan in 313 CE, when Christianity became the official faith of the Roman Empire, it was difficult to be in any part of Europe, certainly Western Europe, and escape the tentacles of Christendom. That the Irish church was always in communion with the Bishop of Rome, albeit critical communion, ensured that Ireland was within the Christendom orbit. There may never have been a Roman imperial presence in Ireland but faith did not completely escape the imperial paradigm. Yet as the church, structurally and institutionally, has frequently reflected the dominant culture, the early Irish church reflected its decentralised political culture.[11]

Monastic communities developed in local centres of population, deriving their values and practices from the Egyptian

---

10. *Ibid.*, p. 150.
11. With no central political power structure in Ireland, the country had a decentralised structure of between 100 and 150 small kingdoms, each with their own king. There is no real evidence for a high king over all. Indeed, the nearest Ireland got to that was with Brian Boru and that was a largely unsuccessful bid for absolute power.

monastic model. The local clan structure of Irish society meant that the clan gave land to the monastic founders and, on the land, a monastic community developed. The relationship between clan chief, or king, and monastery could and did lead to power struggles, and at times even violence.

Importantly, the strong sense of community and bonding capital was already there, and the monastic communities that developed in Ireland were not aloof from, or separate from, the larger local community in which they were placed. The Irish monastic communities were not closed, as were the European models that developed. In Ireland the monastic community was open, integrated with and serving the wider local community. This was a model of church rooted in local community, integrated and active, the spiritual heartbeat of community, engaged with pastoral care, education, liturgy, and everyday life.

This community model had at its heart a monastic consciousness, a deep down awareness that shaped life, faith and church. There was a profound sense of unity or communion with nature. Community was a great deal more than human. Nature and the sacred were indivisibly linked. Kinship with earth, mountains, water, fire, birds, trees and sun were all important and life was lived in relationship to them. Not surprisingly, God became known as God of the elements. Today we would describe these monastic communities as eco-communities and there is a suggestive model of church here for the present. The development of eco-congregations is already under way.

Deep in the monastic consciousness was a robust sense of the unseen world. Life was full of thin places in which this world and the other world were interconnected. As the woman from the Blasket Islands put it, 'Heaven was a foot and a half above the height of a man (*sic*).' The other, or unseen world, was that close. Life was surrounded by spiritual presences, not least those of the ancestors, loved ones, and saints. The latter were not paradigms of virtue and perfection but, in Celtic consciousness, close friends. This is not the other-worldliness of modern Christianity, 'pie in the sky when you die', or the sole object of salvation. It is a sense of life shot through with the sacred, and of belonging to a cosmic community, a dimension that has gone missing from much narrow other-worldly religion and privatised self-help spirituality.

The monastic consciousness also had a strong sense of immortality. This included the awareness of mortality, especially in a world where plague and disease and shorter life-spans were realities. This was not a morbid preoccupation, but an awareness of death as part of life, which included the imaginative visions of a land beyond the sea, the land of eternal youth, and life–death as a journey.

The promise of heaven and threat of hell have, for the most part, gone off the radar of the contemporary church because they are no longer part of the larger community consciousness. The church destroyed heaven and hell by literalising them; and having lost power and control with the end of the Christendom paradigm, church can no longer use fear and threat to coerce people into submissive obedience, promising the reward of heaven when you die. Death is still a reality but the monastic consciousness offers a more holistic and integrated way of dealing with it. Beyond literalism, there is the life–death continuum within the larger cosmic process in which life goes on. We are gathered into the immortality of love.

Perhaps more than anything the monastic consciousness was permeated by a love of learning. The early Irish monks and nuns had access to the classics and were familiar with the art of rhetoric, which is encountered in the diverse rules they wrote for communities. At the heart of the Irish love of learning was the storyteller, 'who keeps alive the sense of wonder; a love of words that blossoms in poetry and rhetoric'.[12]

Those who lived in the monastic communities were not literalists with language. They loved words too much to abuse them by literalism, either in the language of faith or life. In a world in which faith has become preoccupied with conceptualisation, abstraction and definition, which ironically means 'to put limits on', the Celtic consciousness bursts with the power of imagination. Irish Christian monks had no difficulty writing down the great

---

12. Catherine Thom, *Early Irish Monasticism: An Understanding of its Cultural Roots* (London: T & T Clarke, 2006), p. 12.

cycles of myths and legends. Ultimacy could only be expressed poetically with language used metaphorically. The monastic consciousness has been described as 'a metaphorical mindset'.[13] Metaphors may be described as elastic, capable of being stretched, or words with a surplus of meaning. The monastic communities 'excelled at expressing their faith in symbols, metaphors and images, both visual and poetic'.[14] This included the use of myth and fantasy as vehicles of the deepest values and meaning. The contemporary expression of church would do well to recover this dimension of monastic consciousness, including a rich awareness of the power of myth, and its place in the telling of the Bible stories. A faith community in which storytelling, and the making of stories, is key will be a community where God, faith, the sense of the sacred, an integrated life–death continuum, will be creatively empowering.

The monastic or Celtic way with words is evident in the writing of monastic rules, penitentials and the lives of saints. The rules reveal a distinctive way of life and as such are a disciplined approach to living in community. This is how faith is lived out in all the dimensions of community living. Modern individualism is foreign to the communal experience. Individualistic faith is neither a biblical or Celtic experience. The monastic model of church and faith is communitarian.

It is significant that the rules are so diverse. We can still access the rules of Ailbe, Ciaran, Comgall, Columba and Columbanus. There was no uniformity or conformity in the early Celtic church. No one rule was imposed on all. The monastic communities were comfortable with diversity. In that sense they were going against the grain of the Christendom paradigm. A monastic community was not without order. The rule was an ordered way of life, but there was no need or desire in Ireland to impose uniformity of rule on all communities. There was freedom in diversity, and indeed order and diversity. Contemporary faith communities may well find life and energy in the practice of diversity.

---

13. *Ibid.*, p. 13.
14. *Ibid.*, p. 84.

At the same time a rule introduced accountability to community life. Within Comgall's community every individual did not do what they thought was right in their own eyes. Individualism is destructive of life together. Belonging to the community ordered by way of life was to be accountable to one another. Disciplined community is about mutual accountability, whether for the abbot, community leaders, or members. The essence of the rule of Comgall for the dynamic community of Bangor was 'Love Christ, hate wealth; piety to thee towards the King of the sun and smoothness towards men.' This is both simple and radical. Love is the essence, and so too are the relational values of social and economic justice, and respect for God, humans and the elements / nature. There is an integrated wholeness about community life, which is responsible life or shared accountability.

As already indicated, monastic communities were places of learning and many were great centres of scholarship, including scripture exegesis. This did not mean that the monastic communities produced systematic theologies. There was no single, distinctive Irish theology in the systematic sense. If anything the Celtic monks were untidy about theology. Perhaps this was not surprising given the affective or poetic approach, rather than a cognitive approach. Scholastic theology came later; however, theological doctrine was already in formulation. By the time the monastic model developed in Ireland the creeds of Christendom had been formulated. Patrick's *Confession* gives a creedal formulation, which echoes the Apostles' Creed.

The Irish community model did not engage in formal theology. It did not systematise divine revelation. Given the power of imagination and the use of poetry and metaphor, the Irish monks and nuns were doing theology, not a speculative type, but imaginative theology. It is even thought that the diverse character of the monastic communities 'encouraged practical experiments' in theology and may even have produced some unorthodox theology.[15] Unorthodox, of course, is relative to the centralisation and uniformity of truth and doctrine in the Christendom paradigm.

15. *Ibid.*, pp. 20–21. Quoting Kathleen Hughes in footnote 94.

It may be that theologies in the Irish monastic communities were as diverse as the rules. Certainly the greatest theologian to emerge from Ireland, John Eriugena, was pushing the boundaries of theological reflection beyond the known, to the unknown and unknowable; to theology beyond words, which is deeply paradoxical. He was also pointing to the heart of divinity in the essence of our humanity. This is faith exploring without certainty, and with no need for certainty. It is much more liberating than the modernist search for factual certainty, and the equally modernist, fundamentalist invention of absolute certainty.

Monastic Models of Ministry
Celtic monasteries produced a model of ministry that was collegiate and communitarian rather than individualistic. They embraced and encompassed a great variety of types of ministry. Monasteries functioned to fulfil a plethora of roles: that of hospital, hotel, school, university, art workshop, open prison and reformatory, night shelter, drop-in centre, as well as church, retreat house, mission station, and place of prayer and spiritual healing. They were learning centres, community centres, and healing centres, for the people of God. Monasteries practised hospitality and pastoral care as part of their ministry of presence and availability. Monks and abbesses counselled penitents who came to them, and they also travelled into the countryside to preach and provide pastoral support. Most importantly, life and work centred round a community of prayer; balance was sought between solitude and community, activity and contemplation, worship and pastoral care. They were also places of vision where a different world, the world intended by God, could be lived out. As such, monastic life sought to nurture true community with God present in their midst.

Ministry is what the church does in the world, with the world. It is not what the church does *to* the world, or *for* the world, but *with* the world. It is a ministry of presence. 'The essence of this pastoral ministry of presence was seen as a more important function for the church than engaging in mission and evangelism.'[16]

---

16. Ian Bradley, *Colonies of Heaven: Celtic Models for Today's Church* (London: Dalton, Longman and Todd, 2000), p. 15.

Churches, like businesses, produce mission statements and create strategic plans. We organise a Eucharistic Congress, or a five-year plan of evangelism. The assumption is that the planned activities are things we are going to do for the world. These events will bring people back to the church. It may even be the answer to the church's survival! The problem is that the world, by and large, is no longer open to the package. All the wrappings and trappings of the institutionalised faith no longer appeal. A ministry of presence is with the world, alongside the world. It is the faith community being the faith community, not as a subculture closed off from the world, but as a counterculture. It is a visible presence, different and alternative. Presence means embodiment, which in turn is about visibility.

An Embodied Theology of Community
The monastic community lived an embodied theology of community at the core of the local community. The community was, as noted earlier, an open community, integrated and engaged with the people around it. As such, it was a community of inter-action and interdependence. Celtic monks and nuns lived with the people, were of the people, were in relationship with the people, and embodied a presence which people identified with. An embodied presence is not confined to a building but is primarily in community. 'Church on Sunday' is not the essence of belonging, and traditional churches seem slow to realise this.

Religion is the search for God, the transcendent, ultimate other, or even the non-Being at the heart of life. Institutional forms of religion do not always help in the search. Churches can often be pre-occupied with arguments about theological and doctrinal issues, and highly selective issues of personal morality, usually sexuality, but all of which have little to do with real life. In other words, the church can often be preoccupied with questions people in the world are not asking. Life experience throws up ultimate questions. These are the questions of present crisis and questions of uncertainty in relation to the future. Life is hard and often inexplicable. Suffering, disease, disaster, catastrophe, and personal tragedy, appear beyond reason. Individual God-images frequently make no sense. An agnosticism of life and practical atheism are closer to human experience than certainty of belief. Indeed, the latter may be a coping mechanism that we mostly invent. A faith community, one which adheres to an embodied theology of community, is present as a community where the often unanswerable questions of life can be explored and meaning sought.

> A community must be a place where people can deal with realistic life issues. A task of people in the community is to show they are really concerned with these issues.[17]

The presence of such a community does not mean rational answers, or clear explanations, but an openness to engage, or be with, questions in a community of spiritual connectedness and search.

A Community of Spiritual Direction

Spiritual direction was what these embodied communities were good at. Study, reflection and work were important dimensions to daily life. At the centre of monastic life were prayer, liturgy and worship. The hours were observed, five times in a day, and at the heart of each gathering and liturgy were the psalms. Through the psalms those who prayed and worshipped were in touch with the poetry of Ancient Israel. The people of the Hebrew Bible excelled at storytelling, poetry, myth and metaphor. In the Celtic monasteries they were at home with the psalms, not just because they too had a way with words, but they gave voice to the whole spectrum of human struggle and experience. Psalms of lament, in particular, voiced the person or community's sense of the silence or absence of God, human loss of faith, or struggle for meaning. In such psalms faith argued with God, when there was no sense of God's presence, or God was unbelievable. There were of course psalms of praise and celebration, usually when the community experienced liberation from an experience of oppression, or when social and economic justice was done. There was, in fact, poetry for all seasons and the Celtic poetic or metaphoric mindsets immersed themselves in Israel's poetic prayer.

---

17. Jerry C. Doherty, *A Celtic Model of Ministry: The Reawakening of Community Spirituality* (Minnesota: The Liturgical Press, 2003), p. 65.

The soul-friend was an essential part of the monastic spiritual experience and community. The soul-friend was part of the embodied community's pastoral care in and with the wider community. Brigid of Kildare is reputed to have told a young cleric from Ferns that

> a man without a soul-friend is a body without a head: for it is water of a limey lough, neither good for drinking and washing, that is like a man without a soul-friend.[18]

Such was the importance of the soul-friend in the monastic community. Religious and lay people had soul-friends. Spiritual direction was part of life, within the monastery and without. Such a person was a confessor, counsellor, and spiritual director. He or she was by no means a model of spiritual perfection. Such did not and has never existed. They were people of wisdom, practical wisdom, on their own journey through life and who could accompany another on the journey of faith, or search for God. The Egyptian desert tradition impacted the Irish monastic tradition and several Irish high crosses show Paul of Thebes and Antony sitting together under a palm tree. They described this as 'opening one's heart to another'.[19]

In a wounded society, where there is much hurt and pain, even trauma, there is need for 'opening one's heart to another'. Today there are professional services and people will need referral. But spiritual direction has a complementary role and needs to be connected, as deep wisdom, to psychotherapy and psychiatry. The faith community with its people of deep wisdom have a soul-friend role to play as part of the embodied presence in human community.

A Perichoretic Ministry
The influence of the Egyptian monastic model in Ireland has already been noted. The Irish monks and nuns read the life of St Anthony. John Cassian visited the deserts of Egypt, observed, interviewed, and recorded the monastic leaders. He returned to

---

18. Bradley, *Colonies of Heaven*, p. 102.
19. *Ibid.*, p. 103.

Gaul and formed a similar style community. Irish religious connected with the Egyptian vision and adapted the monastic idea
for the early Celtic church.

What is also remarkable about the theological experiments of
the Irish monastic paradigm is its connection to Eastern theology,
and not just the theology of the West. Eastern monasticism was a
resistance movement to the nominalism of Christendom. The latter was not counter-cultural, but the desert monastic movement,
as protest and resistance, was. Irish monks and nuns embraced
the counter-cultural model and theology. 'Today the Orthodox
Church still sees the Celtic Christians as an unbroken link with
the East.'[20]

The Cappadocian theologians gave vivid expression to Trinitarian theology in the fourth century CE. A key emphasis in their
Trinitarian thought was that God was unknowable. There was,
therefore, no theological definition of God, God in words, but a
major acknowledgement that God was beyond words and language. The Cappadocians, instead, used metaphors to express
their experience of God. The primary metaphor for Trinity was
perichoresis, which means a circle dance. It is a dynamic image,
full of movement, never static. It points to the transformative energy of Trinity, where love moves in and out, in mutuality and interdependence. It is a metaphor for God as community, and
community is understood as diversity in unity, and unity in diversity. There is also movement of divine to human, and human
to divine. As humans we enter into the circle dance of the God
community, and God enters the human community to transform
it. The Irish monastic community adopted this metaphor. *Perichoresis* became the metaphor for God, and Trinity the model of
community and ministry.

The ongoing task of the twenty-first-century faith community
is to live and celebrate *perichoresis*. The embodied presence in the
wider community, human and environmental, is to be a living sign
of *perichoresis*. Ministry in and with the world is perichoretic
ministry. This means a ministry of mutuality, collegiality, team
ministry, in which diverse gifts work together in the dance of life

20. Doherty, *A Celtic Model of Ministry*, p. 71.

that is community. Collaborative, mutual, interdependent patterns of ministry, expressing the rich diversity of God, are necessary to embody transformative *perichoresis* in the human and environmental community. This is why the prayer of great thanksgiving in the Celtic Eucharist gave thanks that earth was part of heaven.

> It strains toward the end when all will be as God intends; it recalls the kingdom. It remembers the saints and joins them. It recalls that we are free in Christ: all people are accepted and wanted. It recalls our worshipping activity and ministry, but more truly the ministry of Christ, that occurs among us when we live in him. The Celts celebrated all of this.[21]

It is in community that we truly meet God. The metaphor of the Trinity inspires and transforms us to create and build a community of life, earth in heaven. The perichoretic dance of God transforms us for perichoretic ministry in and with the world. It births monastic models of ministry with resonance for the present, and inspires renewal of worship and inclusive eucharistic celebration, with new, metaphoric and poetic liturgies that embrace humanity and the whole community of life.

Celtic Christian Spirituality

The Celts believed that everything was connected. There was no division between the sacred and the secular, between men and women, or between humans and the created order. This sense of the interconnection of all things, which informed the Jesus Movement, got lost in the Greco-Roman world that shaped the development of Christianity, especially from the end of the first century CE onwards. The uniformity that came in on the back of Christendom reinforced a hierarchical, patriarchal, and dualistic world view. It protected the class system, affirmed man was superior to woman, elevated mind and spirit at the expense of the body, and viewed the created world as at the disposal of humans to be used according to people's desires and needs.

---

21. *Ibid.*, p. 76.

The Celts were in touch with the awesome wonder and beauty of creation. Because God was present in the world, creation was sacred. God was visible in the earth, and in its creatures. Each created thing had a purpose and story, a reason for its existence and location. Celts held that every object and creature on earth was interconnected, came from God, and revealed the Creator. They recognised that the earth, her web of relationships, and the sustainability of life was from God. If we, in today's church, fail to recover a sense of the integrated, interrelated web of life we will continue to destroy ourselves and the environment, unable to see the face of God in either.

Another element of Celtic Christian spirituality was the idea of the spiritual journey. Contemplation was an important dimension of the spiritual journey, a way of living life in God's presence. Spirals in Celtic art symbolised the mystical paths to God. When Christianity came to Ireland the Celts adopted the symbol of the cross and combined it with the circle. The circle behind the cross was a sign of the eternal truth in Christ. Just as Jacob wrestled with the angel of God (Gen 32), Celtic Christians through contemplation and action grappled with the revelation of God in Christ.

The Celts believed God was always forming us as we go through life, making us into the persons we are capable of becoming, if we are open to God's Spirit at work in ourselves, others and the natural world around us. Their spirituality also included a strong penitential dimension. The severity of this strikes us today as extreme and even excessive in its emphasis. We may well be justified in concluding that a lot of it was unhealthy, especially its preoccupation with the body and sexuality. This may well have been repressive but then it is in keeping with much Christian teaching on the body, sexuality and sin. The positive aspect of the penitentials was on reconciliation.

Reconciliation was a core community value. It was the custom for those who suffered an injustice at the hands of another to publicly fast, from sunrise to sunset, outside the perpetrator's home, in the hope that the individual would take responsibility for the wrongdoing. The practice of restorative justice is in the process of being recovered, and is even becoming part of criminal justice systems in different parts of the world. In New Zealand and Brazil churches have become identified with this model and work alongside the criminal justice system. Restorative justice was an integral part of the early Irish legal system, and was practised in the society in which the monastic communities were an integral part. Given early Irish history and the biblical approach to justice, Irish churches have an existing connection with the ethos and practice of restorative justice. Recovering that identity opens up a way for churches to own injustices within the religious system, while also witnessing to an alternative kingdom vision.

The Role of Women in the Celtic Society and Church
In Celtic society both parents shared the task and expense of child rearing. At the age of seven boys and girls were placed in the care of foster parents, who undertook legally to educate their charges in keeping with the child's status and needs.[22] Generally a girl completed her education by the age of fourteen and was ready for marriage; a boy continued until the age of seventeen. There were circumstances, however, when both sexes could continue on to higher education to acquire a professional qualification. Interestingly, according to the oldest surviving Celtic law system, the *Bretha Crólige*, first codified during the reign of high king Laoghaire (428–436 CE), women engaged in all professions: judges, war leaders, physicians, artisans, and poets.[23] Fosterage also ensured the forming of alliances within the kinship, which was important especially for the survival of the community in times of war, famine, or plague.[24]

22. Peter Berresford Ellis, *Celtic Women: Women in Celtic Society and Literature* (London: Constable and Company Ltd, 1995), p. 115. In ancient Ireland two methods of fostering existed. The first was fosterage for affection, which meant those educating the child required no fee; in the second case a fee was required, and the price to be paid for a girl's tutelage was higher than that required for a boy.
23. *Ibid.*, p. 116.
24. Ó Cróinín, *Early Medieval Ireland*, p. 159. Between the 5th and 7th centuries Ireland experienced a number of plague outbreaks that devastated people and depopulated the country.

While Irish women had lower honour prices than men in society, indicating its patriarchal nature, they were not without status and had legal rights which entitled them: to compensation if their honour was damaged; to inherit property, if there was no male family member; and to initiate divorce proceedings, if their physical or psychological well-being was threatened.[25] Women and men were bound by the laws of hospitality, which charged them to offer food and shelter to any law-abiding person requiring it. Women also played a key role in regional feasts and assemblies, which afforded the opportunity to forge political and social alliances that were important for maintaining peace.[26] As women were excluded from men's formal associations at public gatherings, women socialised with each other and created their own important relationships and support groups.

With the arrival and spread of Christianity in Ireland in the fifth and sixth centuries, women and men were equally involved in missionary work, as is evidenced in the accounts of Christian hagiographers. The majority of hagiographers were monks, attached to the monasteries of the particular saints whose lives they were extolling, with a view to elevating the status of their institution. The lives of women saints were written, therefore, from a male perspective. In writing their accounts, usually one or two centuries after the reputed saint had died, hagiographers drew on:

> Native saga, continental *vitae*, the Bible, and anything else they had handy, including other saints' lives … to convince listeners and readers of the authenticity of their tales.[27]

---

25. Berresford Ellis, *Celtic Women*, p. 117.
26. Lisa M. Bitel, *Land of Women: Tales of Sex and Gender from Early Ireland* (London: Cornell University Press, 1996), pp. 156–158. As there was no institution in early Celtic society for maintaining peace between peoples, the forming of kinship alliances was essential for ensuring good relations. Sharing hospitality was an important factor in building such alliances.
27. Bitel, *Isle of the Saints*, pp. 9–10.

Christina Harrington believes that in writing the lives of women saints the hagiographers were greatly influenced by the Apocryphal Acts, which presented women in leadership positions in the early church and involved, alongside men, in missionary work.[28]

It is already clear that women were in leadership roles within the early Celtic church. This was also true of the very early Christian movement. But somehow in both early Christianity and the early Celtic church the role of women was eventually diminished. It may be that the sidelining of women in leadership was due to the dominant interpretation of the Adam and Eve story in which Eve was created unequal and subordinate. This was certainly the perspective of the writer of 1 Timothy at the end of the first century CE. And yet within Judaism there were always other possible readings but they have been sidelined by patriarchy.

> Why must we continue to believe that man was created first and woman was an afterthought? According to the so-called 'Lost Books of the Bible', Adam's first wife, Lilith, was created equal with him – not from his rib. Her fault was that she was insubordinate to Adam … Eve, the second wife, was actually made to be inferior to Adam, and thus were women considered inferior to men. And so it has continued for thousands of years.[29]

Religious thinking is still very much shaped by the negative attitude toward Eve, with unjust consequences for the leadership role of women in church and Western society, but more on this in another chapter. The early Celtic church, though, had a more positive approach. A number of women played key roles in the spread of the monastic model of faith in the early sixth century.

---

28. Christina Harrington, *Women In A Celtic Church: Ireland 450–1150* (Oxford: Oxford University Press, 2002), pp. 60–61. It is her belief that the Apocryphal Acts were widely circulated in the Celtic world before Patrick's era. They were well known in Ireland by the 7th century and likely earlier than this.
29. Maureen Concannon, *The Sacred Whore: Sheela Goddess of the Celts* (Cork: The Collins Press, 2004), pp. 175–176.

The best known are Brigid, Ita and Moneena, who founded communities at Kildare, Killeedy, and Killeavy, respectively. These were women who articulated and embodied faith to their own people.

A significant example of the intrinsic authority which women possessed, in the early Celtic church, is in their use of a crozier. This is usually seen as a symbol and instrument belonging to bishops, but bishops did not have high profile in the Celtic church of the early centuries. Nevertheless, the crozier was a symbol of church authority. Brigid, Moneena and others, including Samthann, all possessed a crozier. For these abbesses it was their staff of office and was a symbol of their authority within the church, just as it was for the monastic abbots.[30] The most significant person among women leaders in the Celtic church was Brigid of Kildare; and the qualities of her leadership have relevance for the contemporary church.

Cogitosis' hagiography in Latin has as its purpose the 'aggrandisement of Kildare'.[31] Cogitosus is less interested in the leadership role of women in the early Celtic church and more in the ecclesial power relations. De Paor asserts that the work

> tells us nothing that can give reliable information about Brigid, the founder of Kildare, whoever she was. What [Cogitosus] has gathered together is a collection of folk tales, many of them not particularly Christian in form or content, probably retellings of old stories of pagan times.[32]

Cogitosus' succession of little commentaries, or morals, written into the collection of stories, provides us with a portrayal of early Irish sanctity. What can we learn of the key values and virtues in Brigid's life from Cogitosus' writing?

---

30. Harrington, *Women In A Celtic Church*, p. 173.
31. *Ibid.*, p. 52. This may well have been part of the power play to establish either the primacy of Armagh or Kildare in Ireland. The two churches were in conflict for most of the 7th century. The personalities, Patrick and Brigid were being used as patrons in the conflict scenario.
32. Liam De Paor, *St. Patrick's World*, p. 47.

The first characteristic of Brigid's life is the importance of healing and working for the well-being of the community in the Celtic imitation of Jesus. Miracles, cures and healings feature in a number of stories. 'Following the Lord's example, she opened the eyes of a person who was born blind.'[33] Again, 'following the example of the saviour' she healed a twelve-year-old girl of dumbness.[34] Celtic hagiography frequently modelled stories on those from the gospels. There are allusions in the *Brigid Life* to changing water into wine, though the preference in the story is for beer. These healings are rooted in the saint's compassion, the core value and virtue.

A second characteristic of sanctity in the story is the strong sense of kinship and care central to Celtic social fabric that includes the animal world. Stories of animals feature frequently in Brigid's life. Cogitosus has a dog guard meat for her, a cow accepting another cow's calf at her behest, wolves acting as swineherd for her, a wild fox and wild ducks coming to her. Many of these animals are at the heart of Celtic myths and legends and suggest a deeper psychological symbolism of the power of instinctual leadership.

A third virtue, a radical ministry of justice and solidarity with the poor, is at the heart of the Celtic praxis of spirituality and sanctity. Cogitosus includes a number of stories that express this theme. Brigid vindicates a woman accused of theft. A man is psychologically abusing the woman, therefore 'Brigid took the chaste woman into her own company and freed her from the clutches of that most cruel tyrant'.[35] By another miracle she replaces a calf and a loom for a poor woman. In a very subversive story she takes bishop Conlaith's vestments and it 'was to Christ, in the form of a poor person, that St Brigid had given the bishop's clothing'.[36]

---

33. Cogitosus, 'Life of St. Brigid the Virgin' in *St. Patrick's World: The Christian Culture Of Ireland's Apostolic Age*, ed. Liam De Paor, pp. 207–224 (Dublin: Four Courts Press, 1996), p. 211.

34. *Ibid.*, p. 212.

35. *Ibid.*, p. 218.

36. *Ibid.*, p. 219.

A fourth virtue is that of providing safe space. Cogitosus tells of Brigid's 'city', Kildare, not only known in the tradition as the 'city of the poor' but a

> clearly defined boundary – no earthly adversary is feared, nor any incursion of enemies. For the city is the safest place of refuge among all the towns of the whole land of the Irish, with all their fugitives.[37]

Kildare is portrayed as a place of non-violence, safe space, and sanctuary, for fugitives, and victims of violence and abuse. The holy Brigid provided safe space, and this would have included safe space for people to resolve their community conflicts and work at reconciliation. As well as offering a non-violent sanctuary for victims of violence and those reduced to poverty and unprotected by kin, we are aware, as indicated earlier, that historically monasteries, like Brigid's at Kildare, were involved in settling political disputes. Mary Condren refers to a story about Brigid mediating between two opposing brothers who seek her assistance in their battle. According to the myth, Brigid 'put a film on their eyes so they could not recognise each other and thereby prevented the bloodshed'.[38] The story continues that Brigid would only give them her blessing if they renounced the weapons of war.

Finally, Brigid's sanctity is underscored by Cogitosus' depiction of the powerful leadership role she held in Kildare. The promotion of Kildare by Cogitosus includes describing the monastery in his prologue as

> the head of virtually all the Irish churches and occupies the first place, excelling all the monasteries of the Irish. Its jurisdiction extends over the whole land of Ireland from sea to sea.[39]

This piece of Kildare propaganda, in opposition to the claims of Armagh, does not succeed in diminishing Brigid, even though

---

37. *Ibid.*, p. 223.
38. Mary Condren, *The Serpent and the Goddess: Women, Religion, and Power in Celtic Ireland* (San Francisco: Harper and Row, 1989), p. 73.
39. Cogitosus, 'Life of St. Brigid the Virgin', p. 207.

she is being used as part of the propaganda. Cogitosus goes on to tell of a famous hermit called by Brigid to

> join her in that place, so that he might rule the church with her in episcopal dignity, and so ensure that nothing of the priestly office would be lacking in her establishment.[40]

This could be seen as episcopal duties only being open to male priests with women in a secondary and inferior role. Yet the work in Kildare is described as a 'happy partnership', and in a fascinating line Cogitosus writes of, 'their episcopal and feminine see'.[41] Indeed the model is spreading to the whole of Ireland, which sounds like more propaganda! The phrase 'She continues to rule'[42] leaves little doubt that Brigid is the leader of the mixed monastic community at Kildare. The bishop merely carries out episcopal duties!

Lisa M. Bitel underscores Cogitosus' ambitions for his patron saint:

> The real substance of the hagiographer's claim lies not in the seeming attempt at primacy, but in the twofold aims for Kildare: that it should govern the churches of Brigit's territory, Leinster and the midlands; and that, more importantly, it should rule the communities of women throughout Ireland.[43]

In other words, Cogitosus was suggesting that every settlement in Ireland that contained a religious professional woman owed allegiance primarily to Kildare, although he is also at pains to emphasise that her devotees were men and women. Cogitosus, and later hagiographers, underline that while Brigid recognised the gendered nature of ecclesiastical power, her particular authority, and therefore Kildare's remit, rejected any systems of power

---

40. *Ibid.*, p. 208.
41. *Ibid.*, p. 208.
42. *Ibid.*, p. 208.
43. Lisa M. Bitel, '"Hail Brigit!" Gender, Authority and Worship in Early Ireland' in *Irish Women's History*, eds. Alan Hayes and Diane Urquhart, pp.1–14 (Dublin: Irish Academic Press, 2004), p. 7.

that practised territorialism, or were structured along hierarchical or patriarchal lines.[44]

Cogitosus does not tell the story of Brigid's consecration by Bishop Mel, who 'being intoxicated with the grace of God there, did not know what he was reciting from his book, for he consecrated Brigid with the orders of a bishop'.[45] It has been a hidden story in much of Irish ecclesial life, rarely told, and only being recovered with the contemporary collection and publication of Irish and Celtic texts like the seventh century *Bethu Brigte* (Brigid Life). Bitel believes Brigid's exceptional position as an ultimate authority among women accounts for her unique episcopal consecration. Further, the column of fire that shoots from Brigid's head upon her ordination is a clear indication of divine approval.[46]

One of the major challenges facing the Christian faith communities in Ireland today is the nature of leadership. For much of the past and the present, leadership has been exclusively male, and women have had to take an inferior and at times subordinate role in church life. There is a growing emphasis in political, economic and ecclesial society on the need for ethical leadership. That this emphasis is growing is an indication that something crucial is missing from leadership in its present form. The challenge to the present church is not only to produce ethical leaders, with the qualities of Brigid, but to dismantle the male control of power, and enable a model of leadership that embodies ethical equality between women and men. Brigid's authority and leadership position was extremely original and significant in the Celtic monastic churches, and is highly suggestive for leadership, gender and power relations in the contemporary church.

While we are limited in the information relating to Brigid's role as peacemaker, the fact that future abbesses of Kildare, who took up Brigid's mantle, mediated in disputes and were

---

44. *Ibid.*, p. 9.

45. This story comes from the Irish life of Brigid: 774 to early 9th century, in Oliver Davies, *Celtic Spirituality* (New Jersey: Paulist Press, 1999), pp. 140–154.

46. Bitel, '"Hail Brigit!"', p. 11.

renowned as women who turned 'back the streams of war', is significant and suggestive of Brigid's capacity and reputation as a non-violent strategist, and advocate of peace.[47]

According to Cogitosus' hagiographic narrative of Brigid, she brought certain qualities to her role as abbess of Kildare. She showed compassion, especially toward the marginalised, primarily the poor, sick, and women. She inspired confidence in her leadership ability; even the animal world trusted her. Her ministry was underpinned by a concern for, and commitment to establishing justice, enabling reconciliation and sharing leadership. While we can only guess at the true nature of the historical Brigid from Cogitosus' account, and other stories relating to her life, what is significant is the impact these stories had on the monastic communities. Through the endorsement they give to her way of life they challenged the warlike, hierarchical, and patriarchal nature of Celtic society familiar to the hagiographers.

There is much in our Celtic past worth remembering in visioning new ways of being church in Ireland. The ethos and qualities that distinguished Celtic monastic life have, to some extent, been echoed in the community relations vision and agenda for Northern Ireland. Community building, respecting the earth, peace and reconciliation, restorative justice, perichoretic ministry, embodied spirituality, and gender equality, are priority areas for the churches. We have only to look to our Celtic past for affirmation of this.

With the collapse of the Celtic Church in Ireland Christendom tightened its grip on Irish churches. A casualty of this was the peace-keeping role and reconciliation emphasis that had characterised monastic understanding of church, and determined its praxis. It was not until the sixteenth century that Christendom was again challenged, this time from a left-wing Anabaptist movement. This movement advocated for the separation of church and state and a recovery of the peace emphasis that was central to Jesus' gospel ethics. The development of the Peace Churches is the focus of the next chapter.

---

47. Condren, *The Serpent and the Goddess*, pp. 76–77.

Questions for discussion:
1. List some of the major characteristics of Celtic monasteries.
2. Why was living as an embodied community so important to the Celtic mindset?
3. What can churches today learn about leadership from the available information on Brigid of Kildare?

CHAPTER SIX

Learning from the Peace Churches

Church Supporting State Violence

Let me begin by going over some ground covered in chapter 2 in order to set the scene. Christianity under Constantine was not only tolerated, meaning an end to state persecution, it became the imperial religion. In 313 CE Constantine christianised the Roman Empire, which led under a successor, Theodosius, to Christianity becoming the only legal religion of the empire. All other religions, including Judaism, were now illegal. What precipitated this shift in attitude toward Christianity by Rome?

At the end of the third century the Roman Empire was led by four emperors, with all the rivalry and struggle for power that four emperors produced. Constantine was intent on holding absolute power and fought a series of battles against rival emperors. In 312 CE Constantine led his army into a crucial battle at Milvian Bridge. It was at this battle that Constantine claimed to have had a vision of the cross of light in the heavens above the sun with the inscription, 'Conquer by this'. His soldiers, subsequently, went into battle with a new symbol on their shields, *Chi Rho*, the first two letters of Christ's name in Greek. There was no precedent for this symbol and, following their success in battle, it became the all-pervasive symbol of imperial Christianity. It also appeared as the symbol on imperial coinage.

Constantine was not so much interested in Christianity as in the Christian God supporting his battles and unifying the empire. Constantine created a Christianity based on a series of exclusions, with a version of one truth for the world. His new imperial church embodied that one truth, and set about defining a version of the truth in Greek philosophical terms, which reached its climax in the Council of Calcedon with creedal formulations in 451 CE.

There was now an imperial church with imperial truth, with a god of battles, and this became the foundation for European Christianity.

Europe became a self-proclaimed Christian society, although often in ways remote from the challenges to human assumptions posed by Jesus' teachings in his Sermon on the Mount.[1]

It was this model that gave rise to violence in Christian theology and practice. Such a model raises the question:

Is Christianity characterised by the medieval crusades, warrior popes, the multiple blessings of wars by Christians over the centuries, wars religious and otherwise fought in the name of the Christian God, support for capital punishment, justifications of slavery, worldwide colonialism in the name of spreading Christianity, corporal punishment under the guise of 'spare the rod and spoil the child', the systemic violence of women subjected to men, and more?[2]

This model of Christianity and its particular model of church began to be dismantled in the sixteenth century Reformation by those who became known as the Anabaptists. Their critique subverted the whole church and state structure.

Anabaptist: Radical Christianity

There has been a long history of appearances of renewal thrusts and destabilising Christian movements within the church. Early monastic movements and the evolution of religious orders were sources of church renewal. The Anabaptists have been described as the left wing, or radical wing, of the Reformation. They held that the sixteenth century Protestant Reformers were not radical enough, as they had been unable to break the link with the Christendom model of church. The Anabaptists chose, at great personal cost, to distance themselves from the state-sponsored church

---

1. Diarmaid MacCulloch, *A History of Christianity: The First Three Thousand Years* (London: Allen Lane, An Imprint of Penguin Books, 2009), p. 188.
2. J. Denny Weaver, 'Violence in Christian Theology' in *Teaching Peace: Nonviolence and the Liberal Arts*, eds. J. Denny Weaver and Gerald Biesecker-Mast, pp. 39–52 (Oxford: Rowman & Littlefield Publishers. Inc., 2003), p. 39.

establishments in Europe. They re-conceived the church as: a voluntary community of believers; disciplined according to New Testament standards; and functioning freely, apart from surrounding secular and even church traditions and powers. They held that true disciples of Jesus were first and foremost loyal to God's rule, not the values, goods and kingdoms of this world.

The Anabaptist movement inspired the development of the Anabaptist–Mennonites in the sixteenth century, the Baptists and Society of Friends (Quakers) in England in the seventeenth century, and the Brethern of Germany in the eighteenth century. In the Irish context the peace witness of both the Society of Friends and Mennonites has been counter-cultural, and contributed to ecumenical and reconciliation initiatives in the north and south of Ireland. What within their particular church traditions facilitated Mennonite and Quaker involvement in peace building; and how do these respective Peace Churches challenge other Christian denominations on the island of Ireland to revision their peace agenda?

Peace Churches in Ireland

There is no Mennonite Church in Ireland and there will be many people in Ireland who have no knowledge of Mennonites. By way of brief introduction, the Mennonites take their name from Menno Simons (1496–1561) who was ordained a priest in the Roman Catholic Church in 1524. Menno left the Catholic Church in 1536, after witnessing violent actions perpetrated by the army of a Catholic bishop in Munster. The bishop's army sought to bring to a conclusion a forceful Anabaptist attempt to restore the world to primitive Christianity. In 1537 Menno was baptised, and newly ordained an itinerant evangelist, by a leader of the beleaguered pacifist movement of Dutch Anabaptism. Menno, through his involvement with this Anabaptist movement, came to the realisation that his ultimate loyalty was to Jesus Christ and the rule of Christ's Spirit. He embraced the Anabaptist belief that the church should function separately from the established and powerful civil orders, whose ultimate loyalty was to the king.

Menno also endorsed the Anabaptist conviction that true followers of Christ had to commit to a non-violent practice, in keeping with Christ's condemnation of violence and advocacy of peace.

> If Christ fights with the sword of his mouth, if he smites the earth with the rod of his mouth, and slays the wicked with the breath of his lips; and if we are to be conformed to his image, how can we, then, oppose our enemies with any other sword?[3]

The Mennonite commitment to active non-violence and peace building has inspired members of this Peace Church in America to commit their time, energy and expertise to analysis of the conflict in Ireland and grass-roots reconciliation work. Two American Mennonites, in particular, have made a massive contribution: Joseph Liechty, who was one of the principle researchers on a project undertaken by the Irish School of Ecumenics on *Moving Beyond Sectarianism*; and John Paul Lederach, who on numerous occasions has visited Northern Ireland to share his experience and insights on the reconciliation process.

There are approximately fifteen hundred members of the Religious Society of Friends (Quakers) in Ireland. The first Quaker Meetings for worship took place in Ireland in 1654, two years after the first Quaker Meetings in England.[4] George Fox (1624–1691) was one of the key founders of the Quakers in Britain. In 1647 Fox began to preach that truth is to be found in God's voice speaking to the soul. In 1650 he was imprisoned for being a blasphemer. A judge named his followers 'Quakers', after Fox had

---

3. Lois Y. Barrett, 'The Fragmentation of the Church and Its Unity in Peacemaking: A Mennonite Perspective' in *The Fragmentation of the Church and Its Unity in Peacemaking*, eds. Jeffrey Gros and John D. Rempel, pp. 166–183 (Cambridge: William B. Eerdmans Publishing Company, 2001), p. 167.

4. Quakers talk in terms of 'going to meeting' rather than to church. There are twenty-nine Meetings in Ireland, which gather weekly for worship. There are also Preparative Meetings, which focus on making decisions on church affairs. Monthly Regional Meetings, Quarterly Provincial Meetings and a Yearly Meeting to address matters affecting Friends.

exhorted the magistrates to 'tremble at the word of the Lord'.[5] When Fox visited Ireland in 1669 he was welcomed by an already established network of Quaker Meetings.

Quakers were persecuted in England and Ireland for refusal to pay tithes for the upkeep of the state church and take an oath when brought to court. Like the Mennonites, their allegiance was to God's kingdom and its establishment in the here and now. Wilmer Cooper, a twentieth-century Quaker theologian, states:

> Since the time of George Fox, Friends have had a deep sense that one ought to be able to live as if the kingdom of God were a reality here and now, and not some golden age of the past, or some blessed event of the future. Along with a drive for Christian perfection in one's personal life, there must be a corresponding drive for Christian perfection in the corporate, social, and political world.[6]

Quakers also opposed war and participation in war, calling on people to live in Christ's peace. Since war required obedience to 'Caesar' over against the claims of the Lordship of God, warfare for kingdoms of this world was held, by the early leaders, to be idolatrous. In 1661 two leading Quakers, George Fox and Richard Hubberthorne, penned the first formal statement, a *Peace Testimony*, which represented the position of the Society of Friends in Britain. It affirmed a pacifist position in the context of pressure to join Cromwell's 'New Model Army' and support the rebellion against the newly restored monarchy. The testimony affirmed the Christian basis for rejecting violence and war: '"Christ's kingdom is not of this world"[7] and thus cannot be gained by the weapons of this world.' The choice is for the Lordship of God over that of

---

5. Barry L. Callen, *Radical Christianity: The Believers Church Tradition in Christianity's History and Future* (Indiana: Evangel Publishing House, 1999), p. 86.

6. *Ibid.*, p. 136. Wilmer A. Cooper quoted by Callen.

7. Thomas D. Paxson Jr, 'The Peace Testimony of the Religious Society of Friends' in *The Fragmentation of the Church*, eds Gros and Rempel, pp.103–118, p. 109.

'Caesar'. *The Quaker Book of Christian Discipline* (2005) underlines the significance of this testimony for its faith and practice.

> [The Peace Testimony's] roots lie in the personal experience of the love and power of Christ which marked the founders of the Quaker movement ... They recognised the realities of evil and conflict, but it was contrary to the spirit of Christ to use war and violence as means to deal with them.[8]

In Ireland Quakers took a stand against the violence that marked the 1798 Rising and were among those who sought to relieve the suffering of Irish victims of the potato famine (1847–51). More recently the Quaker House in Belfast has provided a neutral space for political discussion and a base for peace initiatives and projects throughout Northern Ireland. One of the earliest in-depth analyses of the Northern Ireland sectarian state was carried out in the mid-1960s by the Quaker, Denis Barritt.[9]

Separation of Church and State
As already stated, those within the Anabaptist tradition hold that there is to be no higher loyalty than obedience to God and there is to be no 'political' vision other than the reign of God. It is for this reason that the founders of Anabaptism rejected the Christendom model of church and set about establishing instead a 'Believer's Church'. They disagreed with Luther, Calvin and Zwingli, the other Reformation leaders who viewed the era of Constantine as a time of triumph for the church, and who focused instead on the need to break with papal authority. For Anabaptists, the church lost its way, or 'fell' and ceased to be the church, when it aligned itself with the Roman Empire in the

---

8. Quaker Faith and Practice, *The book of Christian discipline of the Yearly Meeting of the Religious Society of Friends (Quakers) in Britain*, 3rd edition (London: The Yearly Meeting of the Religious Society of Friends (Quakers) in Britain, 2005), chapter 24.
9. Barritt co-authored the book with Charles F. Carter entitled: *The Northern Ireland Problem: A Study in Group Relations* (London: Oxford University Press, 1962). Barritt and Carter identified some of the issues later taken up by the Northern Ireland Civil Rights Campaign.

fourth century CE. Anabaptists looked to earlier models of church for guidance and inspiration. They understood their mission as rebuilding the original church on its true foundation, Jesus Christ.

The Anabaptists sought to recover 'the notion of the church as a voluntary, gathered and visible community of committed believers'.[10] Voluntary as opposed to compulsory, for in the Christendom context Christian identity was a given not a choice. Religious freedom, therefore, did not exist. Every child born into the Christian state was automatically baptised. National and religious identity were one and the same, one automatically determined the other. Sixteenth-century Anabaptists consequently discarded the practice of infant baptism deeming it a coercion of conscience and, therefore, an act of violence. It had become an instrument of the civil authorities and was a means by which they intruded inappropriately into church life. Anabaptists affirmed instead the Christian Testament belief, underlined by Paul in Galatians 3:27–28, that baptism is into Christ and God's kingdom, to which the baptised owe ultimate allegiance. Consequently, 'The disestablishment of the state churches was for the Anabaptists the minimum requirement in a guarantee of religious freedom.'[11] They were, thus, championing the right each person had to choose to be Christian, Jewish, Muslim, or opt for an alternative life path.

In Ireland we have had our own version of Christendom, apparent in the close connection between church and state. For over three hundred years the Church of Ireland was the established church in Ireland. Cardinal Paul Cullen was opposed to the majority Catholic Church taking on this role in the aftermath of the Church of Ireland's disestablishment in 1870. By the end of the nineteenth century, however, the relationship between faith, politics and culture was so intertwined that the cultural establishment of the Irish Catholic Church was a reality. This was to put the Catholic Church in the role of moral watch dog and legislator,

---

10. Callen, *Radical Christianity*, p. 42
11. William R. Estep, *The Anabaptist Story: An Introduction to Sixteenth-Century Anabaptism*, 3rd Edition (Cambridge: William B. Eerdmans Publishing Company, 1996), p. 261.

overseeing key institutions, especially educational establishments. This role was endorsed after 1921 in the Irish Free State
and the Catholic Church retained its privileged position for most
of the twentieth century. Repeatedly politicians were subservient
to the power of the Catholic Church. More recently, referenda in
the Republic of Ireland on moral issues revealed a shift in the consciousness of Irish citizens who desired the cultural disestablishment of the Catholic Church. Add to this the increase in the
numbers of people belonging to other neighbour religions resid-
ing in the Republic and there is no denying the reality that in a
plural Ireland the Catholic Church has no privileged position. It
shares a level playing field with other Christian churches and a
growing number of neighbour religions.

By the end of the nineteenth century the same intertwining of
faith, politics and culture had become embedded in the Protestant
community in the north-east of Ireland. This meant that the larger
Protestant churches also became culturally established, exercising
considerable power in the politics of Home Rule. They were vig-
orously opposed to it and in fact saw no difference between the
kingdom of God and the British Empire. After Partition in 1921
there was a history of Protestant clergy persons holding political
office in the Northern Ireland government. In particular, Protestant churches played a dominant role in education, and repeatedly were involved as the watchdog of morality. As in the
Republic of Ireland, the cultural establishment of Protestant
churches lasted for most of the twentieth century. In more recent
times the reduction in the numbers of churchgoers attending reg-
ular services, baptising children, or opting for a church wedding,
is indicative of the shift away from church in an increasingly secular society. The cultural decline and disestablishment of Protestant churches in Northern Ireland has removed church and its
representatives from the centre of political and legislative power.

Were there other factors that contributed to the sidelining of
the church in the public square? There is no denying the damage
thirty-five years of violent conflict did to the credibility of all
churches. It became apparent to many living in Ireland, and ob-
servers from Britain and further afield, that both Catholic and

Protestant churches in Northern Ireland were incapable of dealing with their own sectarianism, rooted in their respective theologies.

But how have the churches coped with this loss of power and influence? In general terms the churches' reaction has been to retreat theologically into conservatism and traditionalism. Consequently, after thirty-five years of violent conflict there is still no in-depth critical reflection on the traditions and systems of theology that were found wanting. The churches, instead, seem intent on adopting a 'business as usual' stance. This is not, however, an adequate response to three decades and more of violence and catastrophe.

Positively, the cultural disestablishment of the churches has the potential to give church a more prophetic edge and critical voice in the public arena. This shift from the centre of civic life to the margins, then, is not a cause for despair, or a reason for retreat, but an opportunity to revision God, reimagine theology and participate more critically in the sociopolitical context. Being at the heart of establishment has always destroyed the critical prophetic voice. The Anabaptist experience of being at the edge of power meant their membership were better positioned to speak critically to power and be more authentically apostolic. The experience of being culturally disestablished might provide the impetus and create the space for churches in Ireland to critique their violent theologies. Only then will they be able to witness positively to the active non-violent ethic and peace-building ethos at the heart of the Christian faith. Cultural disestablishment might just be the lifeline the churches need to free them to become more fully participant in the reign of God.

Churches in Ireland might also learn from the Peace Churches' perspective that baptism into Christ is a stance against violence. Enda McDonagh, an Irish theologian and Catholic priest, advised churches in Northern Ireland to stop baptising during the Troubles. He recognised that, in a context where the churches had become captive to tribal politics and nationalisms, baptising people into communities that lived off violence created ambivalence regarding the relationship between religion and violence. A moratorium on baptism would, he suggested, be one way of underlining the contradiction between baptism into the non-violent kingdom of God and community violence.[12]

Baptism has a social and political character and in Northern Ireland it has been interpreted in a partisan way. The transnational nature of baptismal identity has been missed. We are not baptised into our tribal loyalties, be they orange, green, unionist, nationalist, British, Irish. Baptism, for Paul, was radically egalitarian, relativising all other identity markers. Contrary to popular belief, a person is not baptised Catholic or Protestant. Christians share a common baptism into Christ. Baptism signifies a person's entry and participation into a new social reality, the reality of God's kingdom of reconciliation, equality and justice. This kingdom transcends all of our other loyalties. A recovery of the true meaning of Christian baptism has the potential to unite Catholics and Protestants, across political and religious lines, into the one body of Christ where love of enemies is fundamental to discipleship.

Apostolicity: Following the Third Way of Jesus
Mennonites, Quakers and others in the Peace Church tradition, have taken seriously the command to establish God's non-violent kingdom in each place. They have, down through the centuries, witnessed to the fact that the way of non-violence is fundamental to following Jesus. Further, that this non-violent approach cannot be abandoned in the name of supposedly higher goals, like national pride, or the survival of a political or economic system. Why has there not been the same emphasis on non-violence in the majority of churches in Ireland? Has it something to do with the lack of emphasis on an non-violent Jesus in our worship?

The Christian creeds, which are incorporated into mainstream church worship, were the product of Christendom. There is no reference in the creeds to the life and teaching of Jesus. They, in fact, bypass the teaching of Jesus and jump from his birth to his death. Why did they circumvent Jesus' teaching, specifically on

---

12. Enda McDonagh, *Between Chaos and New Creation* (Dublin: Gill & Macmillan, 1986), pp. 84–85.

active non-violence? Was it because they were created at a time when the church and state, or empire, were already singing from the same hymn sheet? Was it because the church had already bought into armies and state wars? It may have been a convenience, then, on the part of bishops and the emperor, to avoid any reference to Jesus' non-violence.

The Peace Churches' stress on a non-violent Jesus challenges others within the Christian tradition to reflect on Jesus' attitude to the use of violence and the implications of his perspective for their own praxis. Anabaptist history recounts ongoing persecution of Quakers and Mennonites by other Christians who had accepted uncritically the Christendom model of church, especially in times of civil conflict and war. They did not, like the Peace Churches, critique violence, nor did they wish to learn of a non-violent Jesus. If the last thirty-five years of violence have taught people in Ireland anything it is that violence will never bring peace, just more violence. The time has come to find an alternative way of relating, one that respects difference and understands that just-peace is the heartbeat of a healthy society. It is time to engage more honestly with the non-violent Jesus of the gospels.

Jesus' Beatitudes anticipate an end to the imperial system and the implementation of a new order, the kingdom of God. Jesus chose the non-violent symbol of the kingdom of God over traditional militant resistance. He, thus, challenged non-violently the Roman propaganda that Rome's rule was inevitable, and its philosophy of power absolute and beyond criticism. Those who have been exploited and oppressed by the powerful, and who sought an end to the brutalisation of people, and the earth, would see a reversal of their fortunes. Those who had lived by the principles of mercy, justice, and peacemaking, would be affirmed and see their efforts rewarded.

His teachings in the Sermon on the Mount are ways of breaking the cycle of violence, and restoring right relations and peace. The American Quaker, Paul Anderson, states that Jesus called his followers:

> To respond to wrongdoing with good, to return good for evil … This is not doormat passivity; it is active, proactive,

even activistic. Oppression thrives on fight-or-flight intimidation, and to confront it with agapeic love instead of fear or challenge is to subvert its mode of domination.[13]

According to Anderson, Jesus rejected the right of the victim to exact vengeance commensurate with the crime and instead proposed a counter-cultural act of generosity by the victim, to reveal the radically different love ethic at the heart of God's kingdom (Mt 5:38–42). Also, 'Jesus rejected violence as a way to help the powerless and alleviate their suffering.'[14]

The Peace Churches have struggled to understand the nature of Jesus' non-violent witness. Some have held that Jesus was advocating passivism in the face of violence and evil. Others, in more recent times, believe Jesus was promoting active non-violence and just peacemaking. A sociopolitical reading of the gospels confirms the latter perspective. It takes account of the realities of the context in which Jesus ministered and emphasises the counter-cultural nature of his teachings and actions. Jesus publicly confronted those in power in the Jerusalem temple, who sought to maintain the oppressive status quo. He exposed their unjust and oppressive practices, and reminded them that the covenant required them to 'do justice, and to love kindness and to walk humbly with your God' (Mic 6:8). Jesus demonstrated in his life and teaching that there can be no peace without justice and right relations. His words and actions were deemed blasphemous. Those in power, the Roman military and temple priests, recognised that Jesus' peacemaking was dangerous, for it critiqued the violent rule of both the empire and religious institution. So they crucified him.

Warren Carter, who is in the Anabaptist tradition, indicates that the alternative lifestyle in God's empire is weakened by the

---

13. Paul N. Anderson, 'Jesus and Peace' in *The Church's Peace Witness*, eds, Marlin E. Miller and Barbara Nelson Gingerich, pp.104–130, (Michigan: William B. Eerdmans Publishing Company, 1994), p. 111.
14. J. Denny Weaver, quoted by Callen, *Radical Christianity*, p. 147; Warren Carter, *Matthew and the Margins: A Socio-political and Religious Reading* (Maryknoll, NY: Orbis Books, 2000), p. 151.

NRSV translation of Matthew 5:39: 'Do not resist an evildoer.' He indicates that this translation advocates passivity, forbids self-protection, and urges submission to an evildoer. Not only that but: 'It suggests that God legitimates evil and requires disciples to capitulate to and collude with, not oppose, evil action.'[15] Such a translation, Carter believes, goes against the grain of Matthew's gospel where Jesus resists evil in various forms. Carter offers a more consistent translation, 'Do not violently resist an evildoer.'[16]

Glen Stassen and David Gushee, also coming from an Anabaptist tradition, agree with Carter. They indicate that the issue is not between passive submission and violent retaliation, but an alternative way, a non-violent resistance that breaks the cycle of violence. They suggest the verse should be translated 'Do not retaliate or resist violently or revengefully, by evil means.'[17] They hold Paul also reiterates this perspective in Romans 12:17–21 when he says, 'Do not repay anyone evil for evil.'[18]

What Jesus is calling his followers to, then, is a third way, the way of active non-violence.[19] He is advocating the creative use of active non-violent strategies to expose evil, and challenge violence, in an attempt to recover the dignity of both the victim and perpetrator. The third way highlights an alternative praxis of apostolicity, beyond the dubious idea of apostolic succession through an historic line of bishops, and the equally dubious idea

---

15. Carter, *Matthew and the Margins*, p. 151. According to Carter, the verb in the text, *antistenai*, suggests armed resistance in military encounters or violent struggle. Jesus is against the taking up of arms not non-violent strategies of resistance.

16. Glen H. Stassen and David P. Gushee, *Kingdom Ethics: Following Jesus in Contemporary Context* (Downers Grove, Illinois: InterVarsity Press, 2003), p. 138.

17. *Ibid.*, p. 138.

18. Walter Wink coined the term the 'third way' to describe Jesus' active non-violent position.

19. Marlin E. Miller, 'Toward Acknowledging Together the Apostolic Character of the Church's Peace Witness' in *The Church's Peace Witness*, eds Miller and Nelson Gingerich, pp. 196–207, p. 197.

of faithfulness to a set of timeless doctrinal formulations. Apostolicity is fidelity to the peacemaking and active non-violent praxis of Jesus. Apostolicity, then, entails standing in opposition to violent activities and their justification, from whatever quarter, and in all areas of life.

There are numerous stories within the Anabaptist tradition, which recount the martyrdom of members who similarly suffered persecution and death because they took seriously their apostolic calling. Their testimony, like Jesus', underlines the costly nature of true discipleship. The third way, an alternative to the path of violence or passivism, is a radical commitment to proactive peacemaking. And it is the only way for those whose ultimate loyalty is to God, and God's kingdom of justice, compassion, righteousness and peace.

While the Peace Churches continue to advocate for opposition to violence and war, prophetic voices from within this tradition recognise that 'if a global, democratic civilisation is to come into being and endure' there needs to be a greater commitment to active non-violence and just peacemaking on the part of all.[20] Marlin Miller, an American Mennonite, urges the Peace Churches in North America to dialogue with other Christian churches in their vicinity on the importance of active peace building. She reminds the Peace Churches that reconciliation is the mission of the whole church and not just something peculiar to their tradition. They, therefore, have a mandate to encourage other Christian denominations to take seriously the discipleship of peacemaking.[21] Now that we have political stability in Northern Ireland, and a still tentative cessation of violence, is the time ripe for mainstream churches here to learn from the Quakers the apostolic character of the churches' peace witness, and the implications for a ministry of peace building, both locally and globally?

20. Richard Deats, 'The Global Spread of Active Nonviolence' in *Peace Is The Way: Writings on Nonviolence from the Fellowship of Reconciliation*, ed. Walter Wink, pp. 283–295 (New York: Orbis Books, 2003), p. 295.
21. J. Denny Weaver, 'Violence in Christian Theology' in *Teaching Peace: Nonviolence and the Liberal Arts*, eds. J. Denny Weaver and Gerald Biesecker-Mast, pp. 39–52 (Oxford: Rowman & Littlefield Publishers. Inc., 2003), p. 40.

Reimagining Atonement

One of the ways the churches in Northern Ireland can begin to deconstruct their violent theologies is by reimagining their theology of atonement. How is Jesus' death and resurrection understood by the majority of Christians in Ireland? What sense do the churches make of it? The churches use the language of atonement to explain the need for Jesus' death. But what is meant by atonement? What is the history of the concept?

At the beginning of the second millennium atonement was interpreted through the lenses of medieval imagery, with the emphasis on the need to satisfy God's honour, which had been shamed by human sin.

> Anslem wrote that human sin had offended God's honour and thus had upset divine order in the universe. The death of Jesus as the God-man was then necessary in order to satisfy God's honour and restore the order of the universe.[22]

Anslem emphasised that it was God who demanded satisfaction for humanity's sins. Like the king in a medieval court, God demanded justice and recompense because God's honour had been challenged. Jesus, who was sinless, was the only one who could meet the 'honour price'. Only when God's honour was satisfied could right order be reasserted and humanity ultimately experience salvation.

Abelard (1079–1142) struggled with Anslem's concept that Jesus was 'honour' payment to God. He developed the notion that God out of divine love and mercy allowed Jesus' death to save humanity from their sin and eternal torment in hell. The death of Jesus, then, 'was a loving act of God designed to get the attention of sinners and reveal the love of God for sinners while they were yet sinners'.[23] God's intervention to save humans from damnation, by giving up his own son, was referred to as the 'moral influence' atonement theory.

---

22. *Ibid.*, Anslem of Canterbury wrote his treatise on satisfaction atonement in 1098, it was entitled *Cur Deus Homo*.
23. *Ibid.*, p. 41.

During the Reformation the understanding of the nature or image of 'satisfaction' shifted. Atonement was not so much about redeeming honour, but retribution. Jesus' death was reinterpreted as a punishment for humanity's sin. Jesus, then, was punished in our place to satisfy divine law. Jesus took the place of humanity and died a substitutionary death.

A major consequence of this teaching has been the uncritical acceptance of a violent God. This God-image contradicts Jesus' teaching on 'Abba', a God of love, justice, righteousness and peace. So, did Jesus get it wrong? Is God a violent, vengeful god who demands his own son's death to satisfy his honour; or to show humanity how much God loves them; or as punishment for sin? Is there an alternative understanding of Jesus' death premised on a loving, non-violent God? Weaver offers just such an alternative understanding which he names narrative *Christus Victor*.

Narrative *Christus Victor* supports the view found in the gospels and Book of Revelation that Jesus paid the ultimate price for his belief in, and commitment to, a non-violent God and active non-violent praxis. It affirms that the imperial power recognised the threat Jesus' life and mission posed to the legitimacy of its rule, and world view. Jesus demonstrated that living by God's alternative values subverted empire, and exposed the untruthfulness of its ultimate claims; further, Jesus prophesied that the empires of this world had clay feet, and would not last. God, not Caesar, or any other pretender, would ultimately reign. It was precisely because Jesus challenged the imperial social order that, according to narrative *Christus Victor*, the ruling authority ordered he be killed; they could not risk letting him live.

Importantly, the narrative *Christus Victor* model does not let sinful humanity off the hook. It points up that although the Romans were the only ones who had the legal power to pass the order that Jesus be crucified, they were supported by the religious authorities in Jerusalem, and the mob who chose Barabbas over Jesus. Even Jesus' male disciples deserted him, unable to comprehend a suffering messiah. Consequently, Christians in the twenty-first century cannot ignore the ways in which we, too, have rejected Jesus and all he represents. Weaver stresses this aspect of narrative *Christus Victor*:

> Jesus died making the reign of God present for us while we were still sinners. To acknowledge our human sinfulness is to become aware of our participation in the forces of evil that killed Jesus, including their present manifestation in such powers as militarism, nationalism, racism, sexism, heterosexism, and poverty that still bind and oppress.[24]

Recognising our own capitulation to forces of evil in this world enables us to take ownership of our rejection of the gospel of life and rule of God, as revealed by Jesus, and turn our lives around.

As we know, the story did not end with Jesus' death because God raised Jesus from the dead. Jesus' resurrection is an affirmation of his life and ministry – God's yes to Jesus and all that he said and did. God continues to invite all to choose life and participate in the establishment of God's non-violent reign.

A Christendom church, presided over by the emperor, rejected the narrative *Christus Victor* mindset that Weaver believes predominated in the Jesus community and early church. There were obvious reasons for this rejection. Firstly, it was the Romans who crucified Jesus, using a brutal means of imperial execution and, as the creeds demonstrate, the empire wanted to distance itself from this fact.[25] Secondly, the imagery of Christ victorious set Christ over empire, as conqueror who defeated the principalities and powers. The writer of Revelation uses the imagery of Satan to represent the empire; Christ's defeat of Satan is code language for Christ's victory over the oppressive economic and militaristic system of imperial Rome. Finally, the Roman belief that victory could only be achieved by superior violence, the *Pax Romana*, relied on a superior, violent God. Redemptive violence requires a violent God.

---

24. *Ibid.*, p. 49.
25. The Creeds affirm that Jesus was 'crucified under Pontius Pilate', which softens the truth that Jesus was crucified by Pontius Pilate.

The Peace Churches invite others to stand in the tradition of those in the early church who, before capitulation to Christendom, witnessed to God's alternative sociopolitical and economic world view. They remind us that Jesus preached a gospel of active non-violence, posited on an active non-violent God. This God was not a child abuser, and did not require the death of Jesus as atonement, or payment, for sin. Nor did this God expect passive submission to violence.

Narrative *Christus Victor* is an ethical model, rooted in the ecclesiology of the early church that actively and non-violently challenges domination systems and structures in the contemporary context. It is the model needed to dismantle permanently the myth of redemptive violence, which has underpinned violent theology and religious justifications of violence in Ireland. Viewing reality from the narrative *Christus Victor* perspective would enable Christians in Ireland to profess a non-violent God, and practice active non-violent resistance and redemptive love. After thirty-five years of violence that destroyed lives in Ireland and further afield, the time is ripe for change of theological outlook and community praxis.

Affirming a God of Life and Wisdom

The imperial God is a violent God who justifies a violent grasp at power as domination. The imperial God uses empires to crush those who disobey God's word, and are unfaithful. An imperial God uses threat of punishment, fear, and suffering, to control people. An imperial God demands atonement, or at best accepts the perfect sacrifice, to satisfy honour and punitive justice. Christendom affirmed such a God, and the church blessed 'holy' wars and colonial expansionism, all in the name of an imperial kingdom and God.

The Anabaptists, in the context of religiously justified imperial violence in Europe in the seventeenth century, raised questions. In a violent world is it illogical to speak of a non-violent God? Is it necessary to believe in an all-powerful God, rather than a vulnerable, compassionate God, who suffers alongside? The Peace Churches became a critical counter-cultural voice, challenging violent God-talk and offering an alternative image of God, and way of relating to God and each other. They affirmed that the God Jesus revealed is a non-violent God who encourages just peace-making.

Stanley Hauerwas, in the Anabaptist tradition, believes that 'non-violence is not just one implication among others that can be drawn from our Christian beliefs; it is at the very heart of our understanding of God'.[26] It is an essential act of faithfulness, then, to doubt the authority of 'sacred texts' that legitimate violence in God's name. Jack Nelson-Pallmeyer sounds a timely reminder about the limitations of our God-talk:

> God is more than a human construct, but our images of God are not. God is real, but descriptions of God, including those drawn from biblical images and metaphors, are limited, flawed, and often wrong.[27]

Violent god-images are not only abusive of God, they are also conducive to unjust and inhumane socio-economic and political relations on a national and global scale. They highlight the connections between our linguistic horizons and the interpretative systems we construct, or inherit, that impose order and make sense of the world. A world being destroyed by violence, much of it done with justifying reference to God and 'sacred texts', is a world in desperate need of new understandings of divine power.

Grace Jantzen, from within the Anabaptist tradition, offers an image of God who is the antithesis of violence, the God of creation in Genesis 1 and 2.

> The God of creation is a God of abundance. The theme of the Genesis story is generosity, overflowing of creative plenitude. Moreover, this divine fecundity expresses itself in diversity, an immense excessive variety of plants and animals, stars and seas.[28]

---

26. Callen, *Radical Christianity*, p. 149.
27. Jack Nelson-Pallmeyer, *Jesus Against Christianity* (Harrisburg, Pennsylvania: Trinity Press International, 2001), p. 12.
28. Grace M. Jantzen, 'The Courtroom and the Garden: Gender and Violence in Christendom' in *Violence Against Women in Contemporary World Religion: Roots and Cures*, eds Daniel C. Maguire and Sa'diyya Shaikh, pp. 29–48, (Cleveland: Pilgrim Press, 2007), p. 43.

This God of abundance blesses all and welcomes all; it is a God who affirms creation and gives humans the task of nurturing and preserving creation in all its beauty and diversity. This is a God in whose image men and women are together created; a God who champions human dignity, equality and worth.

The suggestion in the Genesis text is that evil and violence are intrusions in creation, and are problems requiring a solution. 'Creation was accomplished by God's Word and not by violence, and therefore violence is neither inevitable nor part of God's intention for human life and history.'[29]

The creation account in Genesis acts as a reassurance to those suffering through domination that it is Yahweh who created the world and Yahweh will 'maintain the good earth ... despite human wickedness'.[30] The creator God of Genesis releases the potential in the undifferentiated mass to realise its form, confident of the goodness and integrity of creation. Yahweh, the non-violent, creator God, embraces difference, creates space for newness, celebrates multiplicity, and risks uncertainty, for the sake of an open-ended future.

We encounter this creator God in the created world, in relationship with others who share our world view, or who offer alternative perspectives, and in the struggles for life in the face of injustice and violence. We meet this God in the emergence of the human spirit that continues to trust, hope, and witness to an alternative way of living, where justice, mercy, truthfulness and peace are achievable; and where those pushed to the margins of society are brought to the centre.

Elizabeth Johnson, who shares Jantzen's feminist perspective, agrees that God is engaged in sustaining and enfolding creation.[31]

---

29. Neal Blough, 'Globalization and Claiming Truth' in *Seeking Cultures of Peace: A Peace Church Conversation*, eds, Fernando Enns, Scott Holland and Ann K. Riggs, pp. 45–61 (Telford PA: Cascadia Publishing House, 2004), p. 53.

30. Sean Freyne, *Jesus, A Jewish Galilean: A new reading of the Jesus Story* (London: T & T Clark International, Imprint of Continuum International Publishing Group, 2004), p. 29.

31. Elizabeth A. Johnson, *She Who Is: The Mystery of God in Feminist Theological Discourse* (New York: The Crossroad Publishing Company, 1995), p. 13.

One of the images Johnson recovers from the Bible as a metaphor for God is wisdom/*sophia*, a female image for God's creative and saving action in the world: 'Holy Wisdom is a hidden God, absolute holy mystery … bent on the world's healing and liberation through all of history's reversals and defeats.'[32] This metaphor for God points up the mystery of God beyond the grasp of all our limited approximations. The metaphor hints at a God who is intimately involved in addressing the brokenness and devastation in the world that results from violence and war. Wisdom/*Sophia* empowers women and men to respond to human and ecological suffering with a praxis that combines compassion and understanding in the pursuit of just peace.

In Northern Ireland the preferred god has been the territorial god of violence who incites fear of 'the other'; an orange or green god, who has fuelled sectarianism and racism. This partisan god has defended traditional marching routes and blessed peace walls; rejoiced in division and promoted separateness. It is time to recognise that the god of Ulster, and god of Ireland, is a false god who bears no resemblance to the God of Jesus and Paul. Worshipping at the altar of the god of violence is tantamount to idolatry. We need to rethink our God-language and consciously choose active non-violent God-images when praying to, speaking of, or writing about God. Only then will we be able to move beyond the violence of sexism, sectarianism, and racism, to a more honest appraisal of our humanity, and of the values needed to construct a more human, humane, and non-violent community. The key question is: Can the churches in Northern Ireland let go of violent god-images and embrace instead the wise, creator God-images that will move us out of violence toward just-relations and true peace?

Conclusion: An Alternative Peace Witness in Northern Ireland
The radical wing of the Reformation has never found meaningful space in the Northern Ireland religious story. Modern Irish history has been dominated by a culture of violence and that culture has

---

32. *Ibid.*, p. 214.

also dominated the theologies and liturgies (free or set) of respective Irish churches. The traditional god has been used to legitimise violence and much liturgical and prayer language has made more use of metaphors and images of death and sacrifice rather than those of birth and life.

The peace witness, however, has stubbornly refused to go away, and has continued as a positive irritant to mainstream Christianity. More attention is now being given to this witness, and in ecumenical dialogue it has increasingly emerged. It is still far from being mainstreamed, as churches continue to hold on to versions of a Just War theory, or remain trapped in their ambiguity in relation to violence and war. But the witness of the Peace Churches is now at the table. The radical left wing of the Reformation may yet be seen as the more authentic expression of apostolicity, and of a distinctive Christian ethic, in a world of violence and war.

The Quaker contribution to peace-building initiatives in Northern Ireland is admirably expressed in a recent book, *Coming From The Silence*. Two emphases seem to mark out Quaker distinctiveness. Felicity McCartney writes that 'historically, Quakers developed testimonies which are not so much beliefs as convictions leading to action. The Peace Testimony is the best known of these'. Quaker initiatives are, therefore, for 'peace, justice and equality'.[33] The conclusion to the book quotes the early Quaker, Robert Barkley's distinctive description of Quakers as 'a peculiar people.'[34] This is a biblical expression used to describe the people of God in the Hebrew Scriptures and the Christian Testament. It expresses a sense of divine calling, what the faithful community is called to be. 'Peculiar people' are not merely distinctive, they are essentially 'odd', in the sense that they go against the grain of normative values, beliefs and practices. They are 'odd' in the

33. Felicity McCartney, 'Looking Behind Quaker Work' in *Coming From The Silence: Quaker Peacebuilding Initiative in Northern Ireland 1969–2007*, eds Ann Le Mare and Felicity McCartney, pp. 1–15 (York: William Sessions Ltd., 2009), p. 2.
34. Clem McCartney, 'Conclusions – The Social Witness of a Peculiar People' in *Coming From The Silence*, eds Le Mare and McCartney, p.164.

sense that they do not fit the mould, and that is what living faith-fully meant to the prophetic tradition of the Bible. Perhaps this is the greatest challenge to Irish churches, to become an 'odd' peo-ple who run against the grain of modern Irish history and culture, which is also running against the grain of the often normative global culture of violence and war. This is what it means to be ex-iles. The Irish faith community, to be truly apostolic and authen-tic, needs to discover 'oddness'.

Feminist theologians and their supporters are often viewed by those in positions of authority within the Christian churches as 'odd', very often controversial and definitely as attempting to un-dermine ecclesial structures. For this reason many feminists feel exiled from traditional expressions of church. In exposing and challenging patriarchy in all its forms feminists are most definitely running against the grain. What they are concerned about and trying to redress is the subject matter of the next chapter.

Questions for discussion:
1. How have Irish churches bought into the myth of redemptive violence?
2. In what ways are the Peace Churches' witness counter-cultural; and what is it based on?
3. What changes would need to occur for Irish churches to be-come churches of peace?

CHAPTER SEVEN

Recovering a Discipleship of Equals
for the Church

The Marginalisation of Women in the Churches
Claire Murphy has written candidly of women's experience within
the Catholic Church in Ireland:

> Women have been obliged to live their faith within a
> patriarchal church, pray in a male-orientated language,
> confess sins as defined by men, and receive sacramental
> grace in accordance with the decisions of men. Women
> dream of the day when in the church they can live their
> lives as women.[1]

This perspective is representative of a growing number of women
who feel pushed to the periphery in Catholic and Protestant
churches in Ireland. Some have opted to walk away; others have
stayed hoping that the experience of women in the churches will
change. But for change to occur there needs to be recognition that
a problem exists. There also needs to be willingness on the part
of those who hold power within the churches to hear, and acknowledge, the experiences of those women who feel marginalised and disempowered. If churches are open to redressing their
sin against women then a critique of patriarchy and its impact on
ecclesial systems, structures and theologies is paramount.[2] Importantly, if this conversation is to have credibility and transformative possibility then the inclusion of women's voices and
experiences is essential. Currently, the Vatican is silencing priests
who publicly raise the issue of women priests within the Catholic

---

1. Claire C. Murphy, *Woman as Church: The challenge to change* (Dublin:
Gill & Macmillan Ltd., 1997), p. 91.
2. Patriarchy means 'the rule of the father' and refers to sociopolitical,
religious and economic systems and structures that affirm and enforce
male rule as normative and legitimate.

Church in Ireland. The signs do not augur well for open and honest discussion on the impact of patriarchy on women in the church.

What explanations can be found for women's marginalisation within, or exile from, church? According to Hans Küng a number of factors have contributed to the alienation of women. These have included: the establishment of patriarchal structures in the church; male domination in the sacramental sphere; a developing hostility to sexuality; the devaluation of education, especially for women, which contributed to the perception of women exclusively as 'body'; and the political and dogmatic growth of orthodoxy.[3] But what does Küng mean when he says that women have been categorised as 'body', and that this same sexual body has been viewed with hostility? To answer this, it is necessary to consider the anthropology that has underpinned church thinking on what it means to be human.

The churches in Ireland agree that women and men, together and equally, are created in the image and likeness of God. But how is this statement of belief understood? And what are the consequences of its interpretation for women? Elizabeth Johnson reminds us that although the churches accepted the biblical basis for the belief that men and women together, and equally, image God, they also 'inherited a tradition of theology ... that has diminished this core teaching by privileging men over women'.[4]

The root of the problem is Christianity's uncritical assimilation of Greek dualisms, such as light/dark; spirit/matter; soul/body; and mind/emotions, which it assimilated during expansion into the predominately gentile Greco-Roman world. When applied anthropologically, men were deemed closer to the divine and therefore of the spirit; consequently men were rational, with initiative and the will to act. Women's connection to the body, reflected in their menstrual cycle and childbearing ability, was

---

3. Hans Kung, *Women in Christianity* (London: Continuum International Publishing Group, 2001), p.25.
4. Elizabeth A. Johnston, 'Imaging God, Embodying Christ: Women as a Sign of the Times' in *The Church Women Want*, ed. Elizabeth A. Johnston, pp.44–59 (New York: The Crossroad Publishing Company, 2002), p. 49.

interpreted as a sign of their identification with matter. Women were, therefore, categorised as irrational and emotional, passive and in need of guidance from men. This way of understanding human nature raised doubts about women's capacity to truly image God.[5] This ambiguity was reinforced at the Reformation as Luther and Calvin left unchallenged the complementarity anthropology that persisted in Catholic Church theology. In fact, the Reformers went a stage further, tying women even more to the body by asserting that they could achieve salvation through childbirth.

This dualistic anthropology is evident in more recent Catholic Church documents. Vatican II's consultation on *The Church in the Modern World*, stated: 'At present women are involved in nearly all spheres of life: they ought to be permitted to play their part fully in ways suited to their nature.'[6] The Catholic Church's refusal to ordain women on the ground of their femaleness, which the church maintains prevents women from fully resembling and representing Christ, is further evidence of this dualistic perspective. There is no denying Jesus was a man, but surely the point of the incarnation was not to affirm Jesus' maleness but his humanness. The Christian Testament does not refer to Jesus as male but as *anthropos*, which means human.

Rosemary Radford Ruether expresses the frustration of many women and some men at the failure of church to rid itself of patriarchy, even after some denominations admitted women into ordained ministry.

> Most struggles of women for ordination ... assumed it would be enough for women to have full rights as priests and ministers and then women would be really included in church. It is only after some decades of women's involvement in ordained ministry and theological education

5. *Ibid.*, p. 49.

6. *Gaudium et Spes* (Pastoral Constitution on the Church in the Modern World, 1965) in *Documents of Vatican II: Conciliar and Post Conciliar Documents*, ed. Austin P. Flannery, pp. 903–1001 (Grand Rapins, MI: William B. Eerdmans Publishing Company, 1975), n. 60.

that the limits of the inclusion of women within male institutions and culture became evident … We need to take a step beyond this kind of inclusion of women which challenges nothing of the structural and cultural symbols of the *ecclesia* of patriarchy.[7]

She also challenges the myth that Jesus established clericalism with its ministerial positions, sacraments and forms of government, and that the institutional church has been transmitted via tradition in unbroken continuity down through the ages.[8] She recognises that dismantling patriarchy would mean ridding the church of clericalism, to allow for the mutual empowerment of all in the church.

Letty Russell defines church as 'a community of Christ, bought with a price, where everyone is welcome'.[9] In unpacking this definition, Russell explains that the community of faith is also one of struggle for liberation and justice against patriarchy and the many dualisms that typify it. Russell underlines that although we have been taught ministry belongs to the church the truth is there is only one ministry, which the whole church is called to enact. No one owns or controls it. It belongs to Jesus and involves liberating and healing the world from whatever is oppressive and destructive of life. The ministry of the whole church, then, is to follow Jesus and participate in Jesus' ministry of establishing God's reign.

Russell uses the image of a round table to illustrate the type of leadership possible within the Christian community:

[T]he round table has become a symbol of hospitality and a metaphor for gathering, for sharing and dialogue. It speaks concretely of our experience of coming together and connecting at home, at work and at worship; it also points

---

7. Rosemary Radford Ruether, *Women-Church: Theology and Practice of Feminist Liturgical Communities* (San Francisco: Harper & Row, 1986), pp. 64–65.

8. *Ibid.*, p. 33.

9. Letty Russell, *Church in the Round: Feminist Interpretation of the Church* (Louisville: Westminster John Knox Press, 1993), p. 14.

to the reality that other persons are excluded from the ta-
bles of life, both through denial of shared food and decision
making for their community, nation and world.[10]

Round-table leadership is about reshaping the church, its ministry and mission, to become a genuine sign and means of the
praxis of liberation. It focuses on converting people from relations
of privilege and de-privilege, power and powerlessness, domination and subjugation, into genuine mutuality. Roundtable leadership advocates for partnership and shares authority in
community; promotes the full humanity of all women together
with men; sees power as shared, and recognises love of Christ as
the source of power in the community.[11] In Russell's opinion, leadership will only truly be in the round when it functions to make
all persons welcome as they gather around God's table of new
creation.

Feminist theologians are thus in agreement that churches will
only become redemptive for women, and men, if they are willing
to grapple with emerging theologies that challenge patriarchal
systems and structures, dualistic thinking and negative perspectives on women, the body and sexuality.

Another area of concern for women struggling with religious
patriarchy in the Irish context is the apparent support found for
it in biblical texts. Is the Bible inherently patriarchal and oppressive of women? Is it a matter of interpretation? The use of the
Bible to gate-keep women in subordinate roles within church
raises the question: Can texts be found that critique patriarchy
and affirm the equality of women and men?

Women Rereading the Bible in the Church
Feminist biblical scholars are upfront about their religio-political
agenda: the liberation of the human community from theologically
endorsed patriarchy. They are concerned to explore how women
are presented, understood, treated or mistreated, named or
unnamed, hidden or absent, in the biblical texts. Carolyn Osiek

---

10. *Ibid.*, p. 17.
11. *Ibid.*, pp. 46–74.

outlines the difficulties posed by the androcentric nature of biblical texts for the churches:

> Few women who belong to worshipping communities cannot recall incidents in which these texts, or others like them, have been used to justify abuse, exploitation, or exclusion of women from full and equal participation in church or family.[12]

Every female or male reader of the Bible, whose consciousness is raised, is faced with admitting that women in the Bible are often viewed as having no identity or intrinsic value apart from their male relatives; or are presented as, at best, unreliable and at worst, initiators of disaster.[13]

That the Bible assumes the male is the norm is demonstrated in narratives that only refer to men (Mk 6:44), leave women nameless (Judg. 12:29–40), or treat them as expendable (Judg. 19:24–25). Other texts instruct the community to recognise women's natural inferiority and remind them of their subordination to men (1 Tim 2:11–16). Is it the case, then, that the Bible was written by men and for men, from a male perspective?

A number of feminist theologians, unwilling to discount the Bible as un-redemptive for women, have turned their attention to recovering the equality agenda at the heart of the Christian Testament. They point up that while it is not possible to know or re-enact the reality of life in the Jesus Movement or the authentic first-century Christian church, it is possible to reconnect with the liberating political agenda of both. According to Sandra Schneiders:

> The real referent of the New Testament text, what the text is primarily 'about', is not the world of the first Christians, which we are expected to reconstitute in the twentieth

---

12. Carolyn Osiek, 'Reading the Bible as Women' in *The New Interpreter's Bible: A Commentary in 12 Volumes, Volume 1*, ed. Leander E. Keck, pp. 181–187 (Edinburgh: Abingdon Press, 1994), p. 185.
13. Consciousness-raising in feminist theology is the idea that you can change the way you see things, and even see things you did not notice before.

century, but the experience of discipleship that is proposed to us and to each successive generation of readers as it was proposed by Jesus to the first generation.[14]

The main concern for Schneiders is not the role women played in the Pauline community but the role women should play in a community of Christian disciples. Ruether recognises that the Bible's critique of injustice addresses the situation of oppressed and marginalised women in the churches.

> Four themes are essential to the prophetic-liberating tradition of biblical faith: (1) God's defence and vindication of the oppressed; (2) the critique of the dominant systems of power and their power holders; (3) the vision of a new age to come in which the present system of injustice is overcome and God's intended reign of peace and justice is installed in history; and (4) finally, the critique of ideology, or of religion, since ideology in this context is primarily religious.[15]

These feminist biblical theologians are concerned to remove women from the margins to the centre of both biblical texts and the Christian community; that is the emerging community in the first-generation Christian movement and the present Christian community. They are striving to recover the power and authority of women, while acknowledging and remembering their suffering, so that the 'discipleship of equals' Jesus called forth in his ministry, which 'stood in tension and conflict with the patriarchal ethos of the Greco-Roman world', might once again become a living reality.[16] Instead of emulating a model of imperial power-politics, which ostracises those who are critical, even silencing them, feminist theologians are calling the churches into exile alongside the disempowered, which includes women. Only then, they believe, can the churches hope to recover Jesus' vision of a

---

14. Sandra M. Schneiders, *Beyond Patching: Faith And Feminism In The Catholic Church* (New Jersey: Paulist Press International, 1991), p. 62.

15. Rosemary Radford Ruether, *Sexism And God Talk: Towards A Feminist Theology* (Boston: Beacon Press, 1983), p. 24.

16. Elisabeth Schussler Fiorenza, *In Memory Of Her: A Feminist Theological Reconstruction Of Christian Origins* (London: SCM Press Ltd., 1983), p. 35.

'discipleship of equals'. But what did this 'discipleship of equals' look like; how did it challenge the first-century world of Jesus; and what are the implications for women's participation in Irish churches today?

Women's Experience in the Jesus Movement
It is crucial that in assessing Jesus' attitude to patriarchy Christians recognise he was drawing on the liberating resources within his own tradition to initiate a renewal movement within Judaism.

> The praxis and vision of Jesus and his movement is best understood as an inner-Jewish renewal movement that presented an alternative opinion to the dominant patriarchal structures rather than an oppositional formation rejecting the values and praxis of Judaism.[17]

Women played an important role in the Jesus movement, and were among the companies of travelling missionaries, or provided places to stay and resources for table fellowship. The Jesus Movement understood themselves as a 'new family' that superseded the old patriarchal family (Mk 3:31–35). God as Abba took the place of a human father. The new family was not to duplicate patriarchal relationships. Those who wished to be 'great' were not to 'lord' it over each other, but were called to become like 'servants'. Entering the reign of God reversed the pattern of righteousness, and the last, which included women, children and the marginalised, would be first (Mt 21:31).

In his teaching on marriage Jesus rejected the double standard operating in Palestine and, drawing on a different school of thought within Judaism, pronounced that women had rights and responsibilities equal to men.[18] In his endorsement of inclusive

---

17. *Ibid.*, p. 107.
18. Leonard Swindler, *Jesus was a Feminist: What the Gospels Reveal about His Revolutionary Perspective* (Plymouth: Sheed & Ward, 2007), pp. 28–29. Swidler indicates that there was a rabbinic dispute in Jesus' time between the School of Shammai, who said a woman could only be divorced on the grounds of adultery and the School of Hillel, who said a wife could be divorced for any reason. The latter perspective was the accepted position in first century Judaism, which Jesus subsequently challenged, supporting Shammai's position.

hospitality, Jesus challenged the patriarchal tradition that kept women separate; he included women and other marginalised groups, along with men, in shared meals and conversation. Jesus also contravened the Talmudic rule that stated 'men were not even to be served by women', by accepting Martha's hospitality and affirming Mary's choice to stay after the meal and participate in the discussion (Lk 10:38–42).[19]

In openly teaching both women and men, and expounding his understanding of Jewish teachings in his parables to all who would listen, Jesus showed women were as capable as men of understanding religious discourse. Jesus also drew on female images when speaking of God, for instance the parable of the woman who found the lost coin (Lk 15:8–10), further affirming the dignity of women. He engaged women in intellectual debate and, in the case of the Syrophoenician woman, was even prepared to recognise the validity of her inclusive vision of God's kingdom, which included not only the Jews but also the gentiles (Mk 7:24–30). A man accepting religious instruction from a woman was certainly toppling the patriarchal structure. Finally, in a world where women had no public voice and were viewed as unreliable witnesses, women disciples played a key role as the first witnesses to the resurrection. The fact that the Eleven refused to believe the women reflects their patriarchal bias.

The radical nature of Jesus' equality vision continued to challenge his followers as they struggled to remain true to his teachings in a Greco-Roman world that relied on its patriarchal structures to maintain order. The gospels of Mark and John, in particular, emphasise Jesus' commitment to a discipleship of equals that challenged the patriarchal culture. The fact that they were written at a time when patriarchy was beginning to reassert its influence, in some Christian contexts, demonstrates the determination of significant Christian communities to remain true to an egalitarian ethos of Christian discipleship.

The gospel of Mark was written at approximately the same time as Colossians, which marks the beginnings of the

19. *Ibid.*, pp. 31–32.

patriarchal household-code trajectory. The final redaction of the gospel of John emerges at about the same time as the Pastorals … and might address the same communities.[20]

Women in Mark's Gospel

Discipleship for Mark involved following Jesus and imitating him. A central theme in Mark is Jesus' suffering for the sake of his kingdom message. Persecution and suffering for the sake of the gospel, then, was, for Mark, a requisite of true discipleship. Part of Jesus' own struggle involved trying to help his disciples comprehend the necessity of his own suffering and death. But, the disciples regularly misunderstood Jesus. This is illustrated in the conversation between Jesus and the sons of Zebedee, James and John, who imagined following Jesus would bring them glory and power, not suffering and persecution (Mk 10:35–40).

The male disciples' unwillingness to accept Jesus' passion predictions (Mk 8:27–10:52) signals their ultimate betrayal of him during his arrest and crucifixion. It is left to the women, who had been part of the group who accompanied Jesus, to stand in solidarity with him on his final journey. They are the ones who exemplify true discipleship (Mk 15:40–41). The three actions attributed to the women: following Jesus, providing for him out of their own resources, and journeying with him from Galilee to Jerusalem, characterise for Mark suffering discipleship and true leadership.

Women in John's Gospel

Men do not have a monopoly on witness and discipleship in John either; rather the gospel narrated a faith world that would not have existed without women's participation and partnership. The opening miracle in Jesus' ministry, the Wedding Feast at Cana, occurred at a woman's initiative (Jn 2:1–11). Women were Jesus' main conversation partners in three stories that revealed Jesus' identity, vocation, and the nature of faithful discipleship: the Samaritan woman (Jn 4:4–42); Scribes, Pharisees and the woman

---

20. Fiorenza, *In Memory of Her*, p. 316.

taken in adultery (Jn 7:53–8:11); and Martha and Mary (Jn 11:1–44). Jesus' passion was watched over by women, from its preparation with the anointing of Jesus (Jn 12:1–8), through Jesus' death, which his mother witnessed from the foot of the cross (Jn 19:25–27), and resurrection, when he appeared first to Mary Magdalene (Jn 20:1–18).

The women in John's gospel also played very unconventional roles. Martha was in charge of the public aspects of funeral and mourning. Mary of Bethany extravagantly anointed the feet of Jesus. And Mary of Magdalene was discovered wandering alone in a graveyard, questioned a young man about the whereabouts of Jesus, and responsibly gave apostolic witness to the assembled disciples. It seems likely real women in the Johannine community actually engaged in theological discussion, competently proclaimed the gospel, publicly confessed their faith, and served at the Lord's table.

Paul's View of Women

Paul, too, promoted Jesus' radical vision of a discipleship of equals. In his letter to the Galatians, he indicated that through baptism all were made equal in Jesus Christ. He addressed women as *synergoi*, which literally means fellow workers/colleagues. Paul believed that any ministry that contributed to the building up of the faith community was ecclesial ministry and had to be recognised and given its place.

In his letter to the Romans (16:1–16), ten out of twenty-nine prominent people Paul addresses are female. Phoebe was on official mission for the *ekklesia* of Cenchreae and is called *diakonos*, leader of a house community. Junia is described as 'distinguished among the apostles' (Rom 16:7). The text refers to Junia becoming a Christian before Paul and receiving the same authority as the Apostles. Patriarchy could not imagine women receiving so much authority, therefore, in some biblical translations Junia becomes Junias, the male version of the name: 'Greetings to those outstanding apostles, Andronicus and Junias, my kinsmen and fellow prisoners, who were in Christ before me' (*The Jerusalem Bible*). Prisca, with husband Aquila, also had a special status in that she later led groups in their home in Rome. Many of the women mentioned are called 'hard workers' for the gospel, a favourite word for denoting apostolic dedication.

Patriarchy and Ministry

In the last decade of the first century Christian texts emerged that sought to reorder relationships in the house churches in terms of the Greco-Roman household. The 'household code' insisted on the right of the *paterfamilias*, whom it was assumed was male, to have everyone else in it, children, slaves, dependants, and even his wife, subject to him. The tension for the second generation Christians was between the radical egalitarian insights of the gospels and conformity to the wider cultural norms. Some of the house churches feared that if a wife exercised independence in the Christian community it could be perceived as undermining the stability of the household code in the wider sphere. To avoid the possibility of dispute with citizens in the Greco-Roman world, which might lead the Christian community into disrepute, a number of house churches began to mirror the patriarchal structures and ethos of the Greco-Roman society.[21] These shifts bespoke the direction Christianity would move in, ultimately sidelining women and their ministry to accommodate empire.

In the second century patronal power began to be absorbed by designated persons, usually male, in a number of house churches. This shift had serious consequences for women in leadership. It signalled a move away from

> alternating leadership accessible to all the baptised to patriarchal leadership restricted to male heads of households … a shift from house church to church as the 'household of God'.[22]

---

21. John's Gospel was written sometime between the end of the first century CE and the beginning of the second. The house churches he addressed operated an inclusive, egalitarian model of church, with women and men sharing equal responsibility for mission. At the same time Timothy and Titus were attempting to restrict women's roles and participation in church.

22. Fiorenza, *In Memory of Her*, pp. 286–287. Church as 'household of God' is characterised by hierarchical, patriarchal structures derived from the Greco-Roman model of household and state, governed by lord/master/father of the house, to whom all others were subordinate.

What was lost was the notion of shared communal authority and instead these house churches opted for authority vested in local officers of bishop, presbyter and deacon. In time these officers assumed the decision-making power of the community and took control of financial and administrative offices. It then became practice within these house churches to limit the role of wealthy women to providing financial support. Fiorenza indicates the impact this development had on particular house churches and eventually the Christian church:

> The ascendency of local officers thus generated three interlocking developments: (1) the patriarchalisation of local church and leadership; (2) the merger of prophetic and apostolic leadership with the patriarchally defined office of bishop; and (3) the relegation of women's leadership to marginal positions and its restriction to the sphere of women.[23]

Closer examination of the post-Pauline letters to the Colossians, Ephesians, Timothy and Titus evidences this movement toward conformity with empire in some of the early Christian house churches.

Women in Colossians and Ephesians

Colossians and Ephesians were written after Paul's death, probably by a Pauline school toward the end of the first century CE. Colossians contains one of the strongest Christian Testament statements of a baptismal theology (Col 1 & 2). The baptised as part of the new creation are liberated from the old regulations in regard to food, drink and festivals. 'There is no longer Greek and Jew, circumcised and uncircumcised, barbarian, Scythian, slave and free; but Christ is in all' (Col 3:9–11). The male–female equality of Galatians 3:27–28 is omitted. The author does not see the need to change the hierarchal relations of the patriarchal family (Col 3: 18, 20, 22). One difference, however, between the ways the household code was to be exercised in Christianity, as opposed to Roman society, was the exhortation to the *paterfamilias* to love

---

23. *Ibid.*, p. 288.

his wife, his children and his slaves. This exhortation became known as 'love-patriarchalism'. Colossians 3:18–25 speaks of the way husbands are to love their wives 'and treat them with gentleness', while wives are 'to give way to your husbands, as you should in the Lord'.

In Ephesians not only are wives, children, and slaves, called to submit to the *paterfamilias*, but the relation of husband to wife is assimilated into a theology of the church, in which the husband is compared to Christ, the head of the church, and the wife to the church, his body. 'Just as the church is subject to Christ, so also wives ought to be (subject) in everything, to their husbands' (Eph 5:24). As the church is dependent on Christ so the wife is dependent on her husband. The letter gives christological justification to patriarchal marriage. In both letters Jesus' vision of a discipleship of equals is lost in the attempt to theologically reinforce the social structures of domination and subordination.

The Pastoral Letters

1 and 2 Timothy and Titus were composed at the beginning of the second century. The Pastoral Letters reflect developments in the church fifty years after Paul's letters were written. They signify a shift from spirit-filled and communal authority to an authority vested in local officers, who take on both the prophetic role of teaching authority and the decision-making power of the community. It is especially in the Pastoral Letters that we find mention of an *episcopus* (overseer/bishop) and *presbyteroi* (elders). The former had responsibility for the collection and distribution of church funds; the latter assisted the overseer/bishop, instructed church members, and ensured the community's pastoral needs were met. The Pastorals are very clear regarding the qualities essential for leadership in the church.

> [T]he overseer/bishop should be a good *paterfamilias* who has proven capable of governing his own household well (1 Tim 3:4; Titus 1:7 ff.). Likewise, the elders/presbyters must have proved that, as heads of households, they are capable of taking care of the whole community.[24]

---

24. *Ibid.*, p. 289.

The same credentials were necessary for a leadership position in any public institution in the empire. The emphasis was on keeping right order, submission to authority, and maintaining the patriarchal status quo. The church and its ministry were becoming more structured in ways that supported male dominance.

It is more than likely that there were still women in leadership roles, as elders, deacons, and in the order of widows, in these churches. And that a number of the women in leadership were wealthy patrons who expected that as elders they too could serve as overseer/bishop, a role which rotated among serving elders. Further that these women were very vocal, articulate and proactive. These epistles attempt, in a prescriptive way, to restrict women to the ministry of women, for the sake of right order: 'I suffer not a woman to teach or not to usurp authority over the man but to be in silence' (1 Tim 2:11–12). The letters are clear on what women should be concerning themselves with, namely, motherhood and managing the household, for women will be 'saved through childbearing, provided they continue in faith and love and holiness, with modesty' (1 Tim 2:15).

The author of 1 Timothy is the first Christian writer to make an intentional theological link between Eve's disobedience and transgression and the consequence for women, salvation through childbearing (1 Tim 2:11–15). This perspective would come to dominate later church thinking regarding women. The unreliability of women, as evidenced by Eve, also gave weight to the argument that women needed to be controlled and silenced.[25]

This fear of women is further reflected in the writer's determination to bring widows under control and limit their role in the church (1 Tim 5:11–16). This was deemed necessary as widows were no longer under the direct authority of men; the author, therefore, argued their freedom needed to be curtailed. The solution proposed, especially for younger widows, is remarriage and containment within the household.

---

25. Mary T. Malone, *Women and Christianity, Volume 3: From the Reformation to the 21st Century* (Dublin: The Columba Press, 2003), p. 84.

There is a deliberate attempt to thwart the mutual aid system that usually functions in women's subgroups and to make the widows entirely dependent on the bishop and his representatives and deacons.[26]

The conscious attempt on the part of the church authority to control women in the Pastoral Letters was to become a preoccupation in the centuries that followed; as did the need to find theological justification for patriarchal practices.

To counteract this sidelining of women, feminist theologians have been proactive in peeling back the patriarchal layers shoring up male domination in the churches, to recover the stories of significant women, like Phoebe and Mary Magdalene. These women provide significant role models for contemporary women and confirm the contribution women can make to church ministry.

Phoebe: A leader of the ekklesia in Cenchreae
In Romans 16:1–2 Paul commends Phoebe to the Christian community in Rome as a leader in the church at Cenchreae, a suburb of greater metropolitan Corinth, and unreservedly gives her his endorsement. We are not told why she was visiting Rome; however it is likely she took Paul's letter with her. Who was Phoebe? Her name is of Greek origin suggesting she was gentile. Paul referred to her as sister and deacon/minister (*diakonos*), the same title he applied to himself and other co-workers engaged in a ministry of preaching and teaching. The word *diakonos* points to a leadership role over the whole *ekklesia*, not just part of it. The way the title is used suggests a recognised office. Phoebe is also described as a leader of the *ekklesia* at Cenchreae and patron (*prostatis*). It is likely, then, that she was a woman of social and financial standing in her community. Phoebe is defined by her ecclesial function, not her relationship to a father, husband, or other male relative, which was common practice in the Hebrew world. Paul tells the Roman house churches to receive her 'in a way worthy of the saints', as was fitting for a minister and leader of the *ekklesia*

26. Carolyn Osiek and Margaret Y. Macdonald with Janet H. Tulloch, *A Woman's Place: House Churches in Earliest Christianity* (Minneapolis: Fortress Press, 2006), p. 218.

of Cenchreae. We learn Paul was personally indebted to Phoebe and he asks the Roman *ekklesia* to repay that debt by providing her with whatever support she requires. Paul's acknowledgement of Phoebe in his letter is brief, but it offers a tantalising glimpse of the leadership of women in early Christianity.

Mary Magdalene: Disciple of the Resurrection

One woman, in particular, is upheld as a true role model of Christian discipleship, Mary Magdalene. Mary Magdalene is mentioned by name in all four gospels as being among the first to hear that Jesus has been raised from the dead. In the gospels of Mark and John she is the first person to encounter the risen Christ, and in Matthew and Luke she is one of a group of women who first saw the risen Christ.

In John's gospel Jesus' first words to Mary are, 'Whom are you looking for?' (Jn 20:15). These same words he asked of the followers of John the Baptist when they first approached him (Jn 1:38). Looking for Jesus, in John's gospel, is a marker of discipleship. Jesus, John tells us, called Mary by name, just as he had done with Lazarus. This was a call to new life. Mary is commissioned by Jesus to become a herald of the resurrection and a witness to the life-giving and ultimate power of God's kingdom of non-violent just peace, which exposed the violence and abuse of imperial power. Mary is presented, in John's gospel, as a key leader in the early faith community, on a par with Peter, and with an apostolic ministry of transformation rooted in the experience of the resurrection.

Later traditions in the West, in spite of a lack of evidence, conflated the stories of Mary Magdalene with the account of Mary of Bethany, who anointed Jesus with expensive ointment in preparation for his burial (Jn 12:1–8), and with the account of the unnamed sinner who washed Jesus' feet with her tears and anointed him (Lk 7:36–50). She, consequently, became identified with the unnamed adulteress (Jn 8:1–11). Pope Gregory the Great, in the sixth century CE made a further assumption about Mary Magdalene, defining her as a repentant sinner, which influenced how Christians in the West from that point on would see her.

She whom Luke calls the sinful woman, whom John calls
Mary, we believe to be the Mary from whom seven devils
were ejected according to Mark. And what did these devils
signify, if not all the vices? ... She turned the mass of her
crimes to virtues, in order to serve God entirely in penance,
for as much as she had wrongly held God in contempt.[27]

Was the patriarchal church attempting to mask the significance of Mary Magdalene as a prominent disciple to undermine women's leadership in the church? If this had been the Pope's intention he certainly succeeded. But, thanks to the scholarship of feminist theologians, Mary Magdalene is reinstated as a prominent disciple. Resurrection was God's vindication of all that Jesus represented, which included overturning patriarchy and establishing an inclusive, egalitarian model of community discipleship. Celebrating Jesus' resurrection involves endorsing his kingdom vision in its entire radicalism and accepting our shared mission to embed that inclusive, egalitarian vision in our own context.

This vision of church, as a community of liberation in which members share ministry, will continue to challenge the patriarchal understanding of church. The early Christian house churches, the medieval Beguine communities, Quaker meetings, and early Methodist class meetings, sought to live out a radical vision of church as a discipleship of equals. More recently Women-Church is an attempt to remain faithful to an egalitarian, participative and inclusive model of church.

The Origins of Women-Church

Women-Church is a global movement of feminist grass-roots communities and ad hoc women's groups engaged in redefining 'church' through creative ritual, mutual support, and social justice initiatives. It is one expression of feminist ecclesiology. Originating in the United States of America, with its roots in the non-ordination of Catholic women, it is an alternative to patriarchal religious practice. The name, women-church, is significant

---

27. Karen L. King, 'Canonization and Marginalization: Mary of Magdala' in *Women's Sacred Scriptures*, Concilium 1998/3 eds. Kwok Pui-Lan and Elisabeth Schussler Fiorenza, pp. 29–36 (London: SCM Press, 1998), p. 30.

for a number of reasons. It emphasises that women are not just within the church but are church. Natalie Watson succinctly describes the vision behind the naming:

> Women-Church is ... not an exclusive term with regard to men, but it seeks to make conscious the reality of women's exclusion from ecclesial processes of decision-making.[28]

Women-Church was formally recognised and named at a major conference entitled: 'Women-Church Speaks' in Chicago in 1983. Two subsequent conferences, 'Women-Church Convergence: Claiming Our Power' in Cincinnati (1987) and 'Women-Church: Weavers of Change' in Albuquerque (1993) confirmed that the proliferation of grass-roots women's groups constituted a genuine movement of the Spirit within, and beyond, the institutional church. Consequently, numerous local groups that sought to support one another in the living out of their faith experience, together with a coalition of feminist organisations, came to be known as Women-Church.

Who Are Women-Church?
Ruether has said of Women-Church that it 'represents the first time that women have collectively claimed to be church'.[29] Women-Church is ecumenical in its self-understanding, and unconcerned about denominational boundaries, despite its predominantly Catholic beginnings. Open to women of all faiths, and to those with no explicit affiliation, Women-Church is committed to the power of unity within diversity, and to justice for women everywhere, beginning with the church. Organisationally, it consists primarily of spontaneous initiatives that are locally based and unconnected. It has no designated central organisation, no permanent leadership, and no formal membership. WATER (Women's Alliance for Theology, Ethics, and Ritual) in Maryland, functions as a resource for encouraging new initiatives, and for keeping an ongoing directory of groups that choose to be listed

---

28. Natalie K. Watson, *Introducing Feminist Ecclesiology* (London: Sheffield Academic Press Ltd., 2002), p. 55.
29. Ruether, *Women-Church*, p. 57.

there. Because groups are always coming into, and going out of, existence, and because most groups prefer to remain invisible or unregistered, the list is always fluctuating and gives no indication of the extent of the movement's growth. Women-Church embraces not only those communities who self-identify as such, but also groups that reflect Women-Church characteristics. It also includes individuals who no longer belong to a local Women-Church group yet remain committed to its values, and those who are seeking such a group but are unable to find one. Women-Church is international, with communities in North America, Latin America, Europe, Korea, Australia, and New Zealand.

The first public Women-Church was founded in Seoul, Korea in 1989 and its minister was Rev Young Kim. Sook-Ja Chung has worked as a pastor of Women-Church in Korea since 1992. She has said of her decision to pastor the church:

> I dreamed of a small church of women ... a community of equals, and a living church in action in the world ... I felt God was calling me to break down the walls of hierarchy such as ordination, sacredness, privilege, clericalism, etc. I came to understand women's ministry must promote the ideology and practice of equality in all relationships.[30]

Women-Church has from the beginning promoted equal, free, and non-hierarchical structures, which support an equal community. It has emphasised the life-giving and liberating power of the gospels. It has also practised openness and inclusivity, welcoming those from other nationalities, religions and with different sexual orientations.

How Does Women-Church Understand Itself?
Theologically Women-Church sees itself as an exilic community coming out of oppression, a Spirit-church within the tradition. Women-Church has enabled many women to remain in the church, even as they struggle to transform it. There are a variety

---

30. Sook-Ja Chung, 'Women Church in Korea: Voices and Visions', *The Ecumenical Review*, 53/1 (January 2001), pp. 72–81 (Geneva: The World Council of Churches), pp. 72–73.

of ways of understanding Women-Church. Rosemary Radford Ruether emphasises the capacity of Women-Church to be in critical dialogue with church tradition while envisaging new ways of spirituality; Mary Hunt sees Women-Church as an alternative to a patriarchal church that has lost any meaning for women; and Elisabeth Schussler Fiorenza views it as a symbol of the universal church, not a split from it.[31] For some, then, it is an alternative way of 'being church'; for others, it is an alternative to church, a parallel tradition rooted in women's wisdom as revealed by the Spirit. It was conceived not as a separatist movement, ultimately exclusive of men, but as an interim strategy for women's growth and for their full liberation.

At the heart of Women-Church is the idea of women's awakening. The movement is committed to women's full involvement in the church's sacramental life and its ministry, with a particular focus on justice work. In small intimate groups women tell their stories. As they find their voices and are affirmed, they become aware of their oppression, affirm each other, claim their power, and are mobilised to seek change. Through innovative liturgies, rituals, symbols and songs, an experience of genuine community and a holistic spirituality that truly nurtures and inspires, the women envisage a just world. In this just world women and children are fully included, humanely treated and free to image and worship God in the truth of their own experience. Within the movement there is also general agreement about the primary goals of Women-Church: 'the equal distribution of resources, the elimination of racism, sexism and heterosexism and the eradication of violence.'[32]

Moving Beyond Patriarchy: A Challenge for Churches in Northern Ireland
The Women-Church model may not fit easily into the context of Ireland but it does raise critical questions about our assumed anthropology, and traditional ways of reading the Bible. It profiles

---

31. Watson, *Introducing Feminist Ecclesiology*, pp. 56–57.
32. *Ibid.*, p. 104.

the core faith value of justice in terms of lived equality, and offers a vision of a more authentic, inclusive and egalitarian church.

The task of transforming the church away from patriarchy and dualistic thinking in Ireland is formidable. It will require greater willingness to listen to, and learn from, women's stories of oppression and alienation in church. It will also necessitate serious rethinking about what it means to be church that engages the feminist critique of ecclesiology. But all of this would depend on churches admitting they are in error. In an environment where 'error has no rights', and the only position is that of absolute certainty, it would involve an act of real faith and tremendous courage on the part of the churches to take the first step toward facilitating and enacting change. The sad truth is, until the churches are able to publicly hear, and accept, their sin against women they will not be able to release the prophetic potential to imagine differently and live differently.

A shift from a patriarchal interpretation of biblical texts is also a pre-requisite for a recovery of an equality model of church. The general approach to the Bible in Catholic and Protestant churches in Ireland is literalistic, and often engages a proof text approach. This interpretative method reinforces a patriarchal reading of scripture that operates to disempower women. One way of recovering an equality model of church is to introduce women and men to the insights and interpretations offered by feminist biblical scholars committed to the egalitarian ethos, and praxis, at the heart of Jesus' and Paul's vision of God's kingdom.

Women-Church is one of a number of new emerging churches, which in different ways are attempting to connect Christian faith with contemporary experience. This emerging movement is the subject of the final chapter.

Questions for Reflection:
1. What can our churches learn from Women-Church?
2. How can the churches in Ireland recover an inclusive vision of ministry?

CHAPTER EIGHT

New Wine, New Wineskins:
What is emerging in the 21st century?

What does it mean in today's world to follow Jesus? This is a primary concern and motivator for a Christian movement that began in the late twentieth and early twenty-first century referred to as emerging church. The movement has developed in different parts of the world, including North America, Europe, Australia, New Zealand and Africa. It would appear to have surfaced, for the most part, in the evangelical constituency, and been a response to disillusionment with the ability of that sector to engage the postmodern culture. There are a plethora of models of emerging and emergent churches, which makes it difficult to define the movement with any exactitude.

> Emerging churches are so disparate there are exceptions to any generalisations. Most are too new and too fluid to clarify, let alone assess their significance. There is no consensus yet about what language to use: 'new ways of being church'; 'emerging church'; 'fresh expressions of church'; 'future church'; 'church next' or 'the coming church'.[1]

It is possible, however, to recognise patterns shared by the new forms of worship and theology, adhered to by proponents of the movement. Key descriptors used of the emerging church movement emphasise that it is postmodern, post-evangelical and post-Christendom. The shift from a Christendom world view to a post-Christendom perspective was the focus of chapter two, so I will not repeat myself here. Instead I will explore what is understood by the other terms, 'postmodern' and 'post-evangelical'.

---

1. Stuart Murray, *Church After Christendom* (London: Paternoster Press, 2004), p. 73.

Postmodernism

According to Edward Farley, 'Postmodern names a liberation into plurality (from provincialisms), relativity (from absolutisms), and difference (from the old frozen authorities.).'[2] In other words, postmodernism is marked by acceptance of the plurality of world views and subjective truth claims that illustrate there is no one perspective, or meaning, of the world. Postmodernism, then, is a rejection of modernism's grand narrative that attempted to explain the world in the language of scientific progress, absolute truth claims, global ethics and ideological systems.

Postmodernism has its roots in the development of deconstructionism as a literary theory in the 1970s. Deconstructionists underlined that there is no one inherent meaning in a text, instead each reader brings their own perspectives and experiences to a text and enters into dialogue with it, thus deriving fresh meaning from it. A text, therefore, has as many meanings as readers.

Philosophers, like Jacques Derrida and Michael Foucault, drew on deconstructionist theory to develop their own perspectives on the world. They agreed that just as a text has no inherent meaning, so reality is understood differently by each person. Consequently, there is no transcendent, indisputable world view or meta-narrative, only different viewpoints. It is left to every individual to interpret, even construct, his or her own reality, outside of which, for that person, there is no meaning. There is the danger however, that postmodernity as a system or paradigm has become another meta-narrative for the twenty-first century.

But why the gradual shift from modernity to postmodernity? History demonstrates that when our way of understanding the world no longer makes sense, conflicting with experience, then a new legitimating myth or paradigm begins to emerge. A myth is a story attempting to explain the way things are, and justify why we behave the way we do. The need to find meaning in life is at the root of myth.

---

2. Edward Farley, *Deep Symbols: Their Postmodern Effacement and Reclamation* (Harrisburg, PA: Trinity International Press, 1996), p. 12.

From the very beginning we invented stories that enabled us to place our lives in a larger setting that revealed an underlying pattern, and gave us a sense that ... life had meaning and value.[3]

Karen Armstrong indicates, 'there is no single, orthodox version of a myth. As our circumstances change, we need to tell our stories differently'.[4] The story of Christianity, for instance, has been interpreted within the context of a number of myths or paradigms: Greco-Roman (300 BCE–600 CE), Medieval (600–1500 CE), Enlightenment/Modern (1500–2010 CE) and Postmodern (1970–).

The Hellenistic/Roman period was characterised by evangelistic zeal on the part of the Christians. During the years of the medieval paradigm, the church was in survival mode and was drawing people into the Christian community. Then the Enlightenment/modern paradigm shifted from faith in God to faith in human reasoning. In the current transition to the postmodern world, the emphasis is changing from self and reason to community and feeling.[5]

As our social reality changes we need to construct new systems or ways of understanding it, to help us relate in, and to, our world. The particular story about the world we encounter is never the final story; it is, however, the social construct that makes sense for now.

A number of factors influenced the shift from modernism to postmodernism. Recognition, for instance, that the Enlightenment myth of scientific progress was ineffective in solving the world's great problems such as war, poverty, disease, and environmental destruction. The 'salvation history' belief, rooted in the

---

3. Karen Armstrong, *A Short History of Myth* (Edinburgh: Canongate Books Ltd., 2005), p. 2.
4. *Ibid.*, p. 11.
5. Jimmy Long, *Emerging Hope: A Strategy for Reaching Postmodern Generations* (Illinois: InterVarsity Press, 2004), p. 64.

Judeo-Christian culture that good would ultimately destroy evil, which gave the church a central role in the modernist myth, has also proved unfounded. This was evidenced in the World Wars, the *Shoah*, nuclear attacks in Nagasaki and Hiroshima, ethno-religious conflict in the Balkans, Middle East and Northern Ireland, and the continuing threat of international terrorism. Consequently a religious crisis has resulted, which has led some down the path of atheism or humanism believing there is no God; while others have felt the need to defend God and have sought to hold onto theological absolutes through adherence to a more conservative and evangelical form of Christianity; and yet others, agreeing with Bonheoffer that only a 'suffering God will do', have called into question traditional theologies that defend the modernist all-powerful, all-knowing, patriarchal model of God.

The availability of information technology has brought the global world into each neighbourhood and home, exposing us to the variety of lifestyles, cultures, and belief systems. It is now possible to travel around the world in less time than it would have taken in the early twentieth century to travel by boat from Ireland to Europe. This has also facilitated the movement of peoples from their birthplace to other parts in search of a better life, and has led to a more pluralist mindset and awareness of cultural diversity. It has also fostered a 'supermarket eclecticism', which is evidenced in the availability and appetite for exotic foods, global arts, and world religions in Ireland today. The evolution of networking as a model of relating, based on the worldwide web system has, in addition, undermined the modernist dependency on hierarchical structures and centralised control.

The recent collapse of the economy and corruption at the heart of the banking world has called into question global capitalism as a just and reliable ideology. The predominance and power of multinational banks and businesses and concentration of wealth among corporate elites, has been at the expense of the general public, and resulted in substantial public indebtedness. The two-thirds world poor have been the most obvious victims of global capitalism and colonialism which, in the name of progress, has destroyed their environments, cultures and lives. The ecological

crisis, resulting from depletion of natural resources and destruction of the ozone layer and global warming, is a consequence of
the modernist belief in industrial and manufacturing development as the giants of progress. What we have witnessed, and are
still witnessing, is

> the passing of Western bourgeois culture, with its ideals of
> individuality, patriarchy, private rights, technical rational-
> ity, historical progress, capitalist economy, the absoluteness
> of Christianity.[6]

While it is important not to deny the benefits of modernism,
in terms of greater awareness and commitment to human rights
and freedom, and the knowledge gained from scientific and med-
ical advances, there is no denying its negative consequences. John
Cobb outlines a number of 'new beginnings', which he sees as a
sign that humanity is beginning to take responsibility for past errors in modernist thinking and action. These include: respect for
the pluralism of traditions, cultures and religions that see dialogue as crucial for engaging different truth perspectives; awareness of the need for, and commitment to, actions that heal the
earth; holistic thinking that is relational, ecological and non-
dualistic; and the development of models of power that are
participatory and empowering.[7] These shifts in attitude and behaviour, which are characteristic of the postmodern paradigm,
create the environment for greater openness toward the mystery
of otherness, in humanity and creation. It paves the way for
unity that respects difference between peoples, as they seek to
meet the various crises impacting our shared world. And it affirms the need for a multicultural, ecumenical approach to the
sharing of power and resources in local and global contexts.

Post-evangelical
The emerging church movement has its origins in the evangelical
tradition, which in the late nineteenth and early twentieth

---

6. Peter C. Hodgson, *Winds of the Spirit: A Constructive Christian Theology*
(Louisville: Westminster John Knox Press, 1994), p. 53.
7. *Ibid.*, p. 64.

centuries adopted a fundamentalist stance as a defence against modernism, with its emphasis on science and reason. In this period evangelicalism adopted a number of characteristics that came to define it. The Bible, which evangelicals believed in its original form contained no errors and therefore was literally true, was upheld as the supreme authority on all matters. In opposition to the modernist elevation of rationalism, evangelicals stressed a personal encounter with God leading to a conversion experience as a mark of divine acceptance. The onus was on the 'elected' or 'chosen one' to live a life of holiness and preach the gospel to unbelievers.

Some varieties of emerging church are still very much within the evangelical camp, while others describe themselves as post-evangelical. But what does the term mean? To be post-evangelical is to take as given many of the assumptions of evangelical faith, while at the same time moving beyond its perceived limitations.[8]

According to Dave Tomlinson, the primary difference between evangelicals and those who see themselves as post-evangelical comes down to the cultural influences. The faith of the former was shaped by pre-modern ideals in the world of modernity, whereas the latter are responding to their postmodern context.[9] So what are some of the perceived limitations post-evangelicals are reacting to?

Post-evangelicals in the emerging church tradition affirm the equality of the sexes and reject the patriarchal mindset that affirmed the headship of the male in marriage. They also have difficulty with what they perceive as parental styles of leadership in evangelical churches, and opt for shared leadership. They prefer an open and searching attitude to truth, which is perceived as plural, relative and subjective; as opposed to the sense of certainty and belief in absolute truths that are viewed as literally or historically true. They opt for grass-roots networks and local activities instead of institutions, hierarchies, and centralised bureaucratic systems. They use poetic language to express faith because of its symbolic,

---

8. Dave Tomlinson, *The Post-Evangelical* (London: SPCK, 1995), p. 7.
9. *Ibid.*, pp. 8–9.

metaphoric nature that leaves it open to fresh interpretation, rather than the evangelical language of propositions and moral certitudes. And they reject the inerrancy argument that stipulates the Bible can only be the word of God if it is historically and literally true.

Post-evangelicals recognise that the Bible is both the word of God and human word, and as human word requires a critical approach. Some draw on the various interpretative methodologies available to account for the inconsistencies in biblical texts. At the same time post-evangelicals believe the Bible is 'pregnant with revelation', and requires imagination to intuit the revelatory word of God in the symbolic language of the text.[10] They engage the Bible to encounter the 'One who is being sacramentally revealed through the words.'[11] Finally, rather than the timeless theological statements preferred by evangelicals, post-evangelicals hold that all of our God-talk, and theology, is provisional. Religion is understood as a social construct. Consequently, they take seriously the fact that we are conditioned by our cultural context, and cannot think, speak about, or experience God, outside of it. They affirm that as cultural contexts change, our understanding, language, and relationship to the world changes, and similarly our theology also adjusts to reflect the new situation.

One very obvious cultural shift indicative of postmodernity is the reliance in this information age on the worldwide web and the advancing technological appliances and systems. Emerging churches, as well as engaging technology in their worship and as a means to communicate with church members or emerging groups across the globe, have applied this network approach to the system of relations in their communities. It is not always desirable, or possible, for all members of the community to meet once a week, so individual groups form smaller networks around areas of shared interest. The emphasis would appear to be on

---

10. *Ibid.*, p. 112. Tomlinson is quoting a term coined by Karl Barth, who highlighted that revelation is concerned with the self-disclosure of God in scripture rather than outlining a set of verbal propositions or fundamentals. Barth's publication is *Against the Stream* (London: SCM Press, 1954), pp. 216–25.

11. Tomlinson, *The Post-Evangelical*, p. 116.

remaining connected to the larger group while, at the same time, retaining a prophetic kingdom-orientated presence with like-minded community members wherever one is situated.

While all of the above markers are significant, Tomlinson indicates that what crucially differentiates evangelical and post-evangelical Christians is 'how much people actually live in the world of the postmodern ... rather than bumping into it and try-ing to avoid it.'[12] Post-evangelical emerging Christians are com-mitted to grappling with their faith in a postmodern world.

The different emphasis in the emerging and emergent strands
As indicated earlier there is no one type of emerging church, and this is in keeping with the emphasis on openness, provisionality, and resourcing the spiritual needs of the local members. From the start the intention was dialogical, and relational, rather than con-cern for defining doctrines and drawing boundaries. In keeping with this perspective, Phyllis Tickle defines emerging or emergent Christianity as

> a body of people, a conversation ... Only after that does it become a corpus of solutions and characteristics, accommodations and principles. It is a conversation being conducted, moreover, by people from diverse cultures and points of reference, as well as from widely divergent Chris-tian backgrounds.[13]

At heart it is post-denominational, welcoming Christians from various church traditions, those on the edge of church, and those with no church affiliation or experience of church who are seeking to deepen their spirituality.

Various models of emerging church abound. Developing out of the house church movement, some established non-denomin-ational churches, others formed house communities around a new monastic vision, while others had no site and located in halls, pubs, coffee shops, and parks.

---

12. *Ibid.*, p. 140.
13. Phyllis Tickle, *The Great Emergence: How Christianity is Changing and Why* (Grand Rapids: Baker Books, 2008), p. 104.

An example of non-denominational church in the emerging tradition that is more or less traditionally structured is the Vineyard Association of Churches, which has various networks throughout Ireland. One of its founders, John Wimber, who was a former Quaker, came up with the idea that it should be left to individuals to decide how much they wished to identify with the centre, or place of authority, in the church. What was important, however, was the sharing of a kingdom of God vision amongst members and a desire to realise the kingdom in their locale. In Northern Ireland there are Vineyard Churches in Belfast, Dungannon, Portadown and Coleraine. They have their roots in evangelical and Pentecostal movements and emphasise connection and community.

The New Monastics are house communities made up of individuals who choose to live together with the purpose of witnessing to Christ's commandment to love God and neighbour. They relocate to places on the fringes of cities or towns, where they can live and pray together in community, learning from the marginalised what it means to struggle with poverty, violence and disempowerment. Some communities practise what is called a 'common purse', sharing what income they generate to cover living expenses and giving what remains to those in need. They also 'wage peace' by operating an open-door policy, which means anyone can join them for shared meals or celebrations, viewing hospitality as a way of breaking down communal walls of hostility.[14]

New forms of emerging church that develop around alternative worship communities, or café church models, or new age communities, to cite a few examples, share an interest in finding a particular spirituality that connects with postmodern culture. According to Ian Mobsby emerging churches in Britain are

> attempting to do 'worship, mission and community' in a culture driven by individualism, consumption, information technology and an increased interest in holistic

---

14. Jonathan Wilson-Hartgrove, *New Monasticism: What It Has To Say To Today's Church*, (Grand Rapids: Brazos Press, 2008), p. 114.

spirituality. *But* – on top of this – emerging churches are attempting to engage with the complexity of particular localities.[15]

Unlike traditional churches, which require members' adherence to particular doctrinal beliefs that inform behaviour before they can be said to belong, emerging/emergent Christians welcome anyone who feels drawn to the group. And there is no onus on any individual to behave in a particular way, or believe what others may hold in the group.

Tickle helpfully explains the distinction that is developing in the North American context between emerging and emergent strands of the movement.[16] Emerging Christians, like Dan Kimball and Erwin McManus, retain the evangelical emphasis on scripture as the primary authority. Emergent Christians, while not denying the importance of the Bible, choose to discern truth through an aesthetic response to the world around them and the community to which they belong; in other words, a spiritually or emotionally moving experience is perceived as authoritative, and understood as the window through which God 'warms the soul' and engages the heart. Christians like Brian McLaren, Doug Pagitt and Peter Rollins would tend toward this perspective. That is not to deny that the ideal is an integration of the two responses, which some within the movement strive for.

Core practices of emerging churches
Emerging churches, in spite of their diversity, share a number of core practices. Gibbs and Bolger outline three core practices common among emerging churches that take postmodernity seriously, along with six other practices derived from these. These latter characteristics may, or may not, be obvious in each emerging model.[17]

---

15. Ian Mobsby, 'The Emerging Church in the UK: Personal Reflections', *Emerging Church* [website] <http://www.emergingchurch.info/reflection/ianmobsby2/index.htm> accessed 23 July 2010.
16. Tickle, *The Great Emergence*, pp. 145–150.
17. Eddie Gibbs and Ryan K. Bolger, *Emerging Churches: Creating Christian Community in Postmodern Cultures* (London: SPCK, 2006), p. 45.

The three core practices are: relating to Jesus' life, transforming secular space, and creating and living community. Emerging church adherents recognise that Jesus created an alternative social order premised on serving others and showing forgiveness, thus challenging the temple movement of his day. Community for emerging church members has to be counter-cultural, resisting dominant models of power. They intentionally create places where stories, struggles and doubts can be shared. These communities are small, missional, and offer space for each individual to participate. Emerging churches form tight communities. It is through living as a community that emerging churches practice the way of Jesus in all realms of culture.[18] The six additional activities that flow out of the core vision involve:

1) Welcoming the stranger, including those of other faiths and cultures, by showing hospitality as Jesus did;
2) Serving others in the surrounding neighbourhood and worldwide with generosity of spirit, by sharing individual talents and economic resources;
3) Participating as producers in all activities, whether worship, discussions, community life, outreach activities;
4) Drawing on one's own creativity, as a person in God the creator's image, to imaginatively enrich worship, the life of the community, and one's own spirit, to receive God's revelation;
5) Leading as a body that is informed by the servant model of leadership demonstrated by Jesus, which empowered all and sought to connect with people, and not control them;
6) And participating in spiritual activities that are both corporate and personal involving the whole person, mind and body, to deepen one's relationship with God and others.

Identifying with Jesus, emerging church members form networks of resistance that challenge patriarchy, economic and social injustices, and ecological abuses. They recognise the importance

---

18. *Ibid.*, p. 155.

of letting go old loyalties like nationalism, individualism, and consumerism that are in opposition to the kingdom ethos.[19]

The Christian narrative of emerging church is a contrast story that challenges hierarchical structures, domination systems and 'power over' models of relating, which informed cultural practices in the modernist context. Underscoring the equality of all, by recovering the Reformation and Vatican II emphasis on 'priesthood of all believers', counters the private/public and secular/sacred dualisms. These latter were a legacy of modernity that led to the fragmentation of society; assuring control and order were in the hands of Western, male, religious, political and social elites.

For emerging churches, then, the concern is not with starting new churches, or holding church meetings, but the practice of community formation that has at its heart the kingdom values of Jesus. Regarding leadership in these emerging churches, while the emphasis is on full community participation, the named leaders or founders would appear to be, for the most part, male. It would appear there is still some way to go in realising the equality agenda.

Ikon: Living Faithfully in the Northern Ireland Context
The Ikon community is an example of emerging church in Belfast, although its founder, Peter Rollins, is uncomfortable with the term. His intention was not to create another religious grouping in a place overrun with separate church traditions. Instead Rollins sought to find creative ways of challenging and revitalising existing religious traditions and promoting reconciliation between them. According to Rollins, Ikon:

> was originally an experimental project dedicated to exploring the relationship between mysticism and postmodern thought in a liturgical context and has since developed into an important model for those who are seeking to rethink the structure of religious communities in a contemporary environment.[20]

---

19. *Ibid.*, p. 91.
20. Peter Rollins, *How (Not) To Speak Of God*, (London: SPCK, 2006), p. xiv.

Ikon is not attempting to be an alternative church but is creating the space for members to recover the critical edge, and radical insights, often lost when any new movement becomes institutionalised. In a sectarian society, the Ikon community includes individuals with roots in both the Catholic and Protestant traditions, as well as those who are coming from an atheist perspective. Their journey as a community, Rollins recognises, is not a foray into new territory, although it is new for the evangelical constituency, but a rediscovery of the mystical insights that have informed Christianity in both the *kataphatic* and *apophatic* traditions.[21] Emerging conversations, therefore

> are not explicitly attempting to construct or unearth a different set of beliefs that would somehow be more appropriate in today's context, but rather, they are looking at the way in which we hold the beliefs that we already have.[22]

The group meet in a city centre pub to converse, reflect on faith, and worship, 'blending live music, visual imagery, soundscapes, theatre, ritual and reflection to create what they call "transformance art".'[23] The intention is to create a space where participants can set aside the various identities that define them and, as a gathering of equals, share stories, struggles, and rituals that help them respond to one another in a Christ-like way. The intention behind encounters, worship, and shared activities, is to rupture presuppositions and perspectives on life, faith and doctrine held by members, and 'stretch language to its limits', to encourage a rethinking and doubting of received perspectives. Self-questioning and 'militant doubting' is understood as a necessary stage in the process of searching for, and affirming, the deeper

---

21. The *kataphatic* tradition is the 'way of affirmation' and emphasises the revelation of God apparent in the beauty of creation, biblical texts, and human interaction, while the *apophatic* tradition or the 'way of negation' stresses that the glory of God remains concealed, hidden from view and is unknowable.

22. Rollins, *How (Not) To Speak Of God*, p. 7.

23. *Ikon* [website] <http://www.peterrollins.net/about.html> accessed 21 July 2010.

truths of life, experienced by Christ in his death and affirmed in his resurrection.[24] Ikon holds that any disclosure of God is mediated through human interaction. This is in keeping with John Taylor's perspective outlined a generation ago in his book *The Go-Between God*.

Leadership within the group is shared to encourage members to contribute from their giftedness. Those who organise the gathering, therefore, refuse to assume the place of power that encourages an unhealthy dependency. The leadership team focuses instead on nurturing relationships developing within the group. This is in keeping with the servant model of leadership demonstrated by Jesus, who sought out the excluded and not the powerful, who sought to empower others and not claim power for himself, who recognised that real change and transformation will come from the grass roots up. This perspective thus affirms that the Christian 'system' actively seeks to identify with the powerless and the voiceless.[25]

Ikon community members adopt a devotional approach to biblical texts. This narrative approach to story focuses on assisting the reader to interact with characters in the text, debate the contrasting or conflicting perspectives, fill out the gaps in the storyline, and discover fresh meaning for their own lives that is transformative. The intention is not to get caught up in the conflicts that arise within the story but to encounter the word of God that is an event, and not an academic exercise of interpretation.

> Word of God refers to what the believer encounters as a presence exploding from the heart of the text, a presence that can never be captured in some confession of faith or creedal formation …[26]

Ikon indicate that the purpose of engaging the biblical narratives is to feel God's word, allow the experience to confront us with our unfaithfulness, and transform us to love God, and others,

---

24. Peter Rollins, *The Fidelity of Betrayal: Towards A Church Beyond Belief* (London: SPCK, 2008), pp. 174–175.
25. *Ibid.*, pp. 169–170.
26. *Ibid.*, p. 55.

in a more honest, Christ-like way. Rollins' perspective that Jesus' parables are designed to confront us with the truth of who we are, and how we should interact with the world in light of God's kingdom, is informative. Rollins' experiential approach is valid and creative, a way to deepen faith at a personal level and influence personal actions. It could be enhanced by engaging other insightful approaches to the biblical texts; for instance, a sociopolitical critique, which takes seriously the critical-prophetic Jewish tradition that Jesus was in, and his concern to transform unjust sociopolitical, and economic, systems and structures. A sociopolitical critique also helps readers to recognise the extent of the subversiveness Jesus is calling for in his parables. To cite a few examples, the Parable of the Vine-growers in Mark 12:1–12 is concerned with exposing the spiral of violence, and raises the question: what approach is in keeping with kingdom ethics? The Parable of the Lost Son in Luke 15:11–32, challenges patriarchy, which assumed the rule of the father was ultimate.

The strength of Ikon is twofold. It creates an environment where doubt is viewed as healthy and necessary for owning our material reality, vulnerability and limitedness. It also nourishes people's spirits and imaginations in rituals and worship that engage the whole person. Like the Jewish tradition of prayer referred to in chapter 3, it is rooted in real experience and recognises that lament is a necessary antidote to praise. The worship, discussions and activities provide a resource and channel for processing the issues, uncertainties, and challenges thrown up by postmodern living. They also help create inclusive community in a world of dislocation, isolation and loneliness.

Fresh Expressions of Church – Anglican and Methodist

Fresh Expressions are, according to Archbishop Rowan Williams, 'mixed economy' models of church that combine traditional and emerging church features, with the emerging strand attempting to connect to the postmodern context, and the traditional element retaining a foot firmly in the world of modernity. Fresh Expressions refers to existing churches seeking renewal, as well as new forms of church that are contextual. The term was coined by the Church of England report, *Mission-Shaped Church: Church planting and fresh expressions of church in a changing context* (2004). It was initiated in 2005 by the Archbishops of Canterbury and York, with the Methodist Council, and since then the United Reformed Church has become involved. Currently there are approximately three hundred new congregations with twenty thousand members, and Fresh Expressions' goal is 'to create around ten thousand new worshipping communities across the UK within the next decade'.[27] The phrase used in the report to describe the development of these communities is 'church planting', understood as

> the process by which a seed of the life and message of Jesus embodied by a community of Christians is immersed for mission reasons in a particular culture or geographical context. The intentional consequence is that it roots there, coming to life as a new indigenous body of Christian disciples well suited to continue in mission.[28]

As with the emerging/emergent movement, Fresh Expressions is a response, in part, to reach both churched and dechurched; the latter referring to those who have left church because of negative experiences and disillusionment with existing models. The Church of England report identifies a number of different types of Fresh Expressions, these include: alternative worship communities, base ecclesial communities, café church, and churches arising out of community initiatives.

The alternative worship communities appear to have most in common with the emerging/emergent models. They are self-consciously post-denominational, and postmodern, adopting a multimedia approach, local and contextual, with a strong focus on community. The base ecclesial communities originated in Latin America in the 1950s and developed worldwide. What they share

---

27. *The Church of England* [website] <http://www.cofe.anglican.org/info/yearreview/dec05/freshexpressions.html> accessed 24 July 2010
28. Church of England Report, *Mission-Shaped Church: Church planting and fresh expressions of church in a changing context* (London: Church House Publishing, 2004), p. 32.

with some emerging/emergent churches is an emphasis on radical justice, which entails preaching a gospel of liberation to the poor and marginalised, and challenging oppressive systems. Café church, like some emerging/emergent models, meets in alternative spaces, such as cafes, pubs and community centres. It emphasises community, discussion and interaction, and practises informal worship. Churches arising out of community initiatives are planted in areas of social deprivation, where individuals have little or no experience of church. Local needs determine the way these churches develop and the community sets the agenda. Again there are resonances with emerging/emergent variety of churches.

Bishop Graham Clay is leader of the Fresh Expressions team, which was established to service the planting and resourcing of these new models. Part of this resourcing includes a well-developed website that defines Fresh Expressions as: missional in that it serves people outside church, incarnational or inculturated, educational with a focus on making disciples, and ecclesial as it is forming church.[29]

The diversity of these expressions of church is a positive; however, to what extent are these models an extension of institutional forms of religion in different packaging? To put it another way, although the models are being developed at grass roots, are those who take the lead in these developments critical of Christendom models of church that over-identify with systems and structures of power and economic capitalism? Also, is the success of mission being measured according to the numbers of 'bums on seats', even though these seats are not pews? Or is success understood as fresh insights into the meaning of the kingdom message and experience reinterpreted from the perspective of those coming from the underside, or margins, of society? The answers to these questions are not clear.

---

29. See *Fresh Expressions* [website]
<http://www.freshexpressions.org.uk/about/whatis>

Church Without Walls – Church of Scotland

As with Fresh Expressions, Church Without Walls evolved from an institutional church, in this instance the Church of Scotland, responding to the missionary impetus to find new ways of reaching people and making sense of the gospel in the twenty-first century. The *Church without Walls* report published in 2001 outlines the church's objectives to move:

1. From church focus to Christ focus
   – following Jesus to see what church forms round him.

2. From settled church to church as a movement
   – going where people are rather than waiting for people to come.

3. From a culture of guilt to a culture of grace
   – freeing people to love and be loved while not counting the cost.

4. From running congregations to building communities
   – working towards a relational reformation.

5. From isolation to interdependence
   – encouraging churches to work together.

6. From individualism to teamwork
   – seeing teamwork as essential to all ministry.

7. From top down church to upside down church
   – putting the local church at the centre of the agenda.

8. From centralised resources to development resources
   – releasing funds to encourage local vision.

9. From faith as security to faith as risk
   – looking for new courage to break out of old routines.[30]

In the last nine years a number of conferences, public events and activities have taken place to realise these objectives, and help individuals, and congregations, rediscover what it means to follow Christ. In 2006 the Church of Scotland General Assembly set up a Planning Group to continue this work of renewal.

---

30. These objectives appear in the summary version of the *Church Without Walls* report <http://www.churchofscotland.org.uk/churchwithout-walls/index.htm> accessed 24 July 2010.

A variety of projects have developed at grass roots throughout Scotland that reach into local communities, addressing real needs, in response to the gospel imperative to love one another. To name just a few: in Edinburgh the Greyfriars Community Project reaches out and cares for those struggling with homelessness, and living with HIV / AIDS; Faith in Community in Glasgow tackles the injustice of poverty, and their community development teams are working in the thirty-six poorest parishes of Glasgow; the Spark Initiative, in the region of Irvine and Kilmarnock, is a befriending service for vulnerable adults between sixteen and sixty; in Dundee a Family Support Ministry operates from St Andrew's church, helping teenage mums and their children with health issues, employment skills, and personal development work; and finally, the Iona Community operates the Jacob Project nationally, rehabilitating ex-offenders through support in housing and unemployment. These examples demonstrate the Church of Scotland's commitment to connect with the marginalised and suffering, as a way of living the gospel values.

In 2008 the Church of Scotland Assembly instructed the Planning Group to create a mission strategy for 2009. It seems fitting that churches in Scotland developed this as a focus, as in 2010 representatives from churches around the world met in Edinburgh to discuss 'Witnessing to Christ Today', thus marking the hundredth anniversary of the Edinburgh Missionary Conference, which sowed the seeds of the twentieth-century Ecumenical Movement. The Church of Scotland Planning Committee developed a project entitled World Without Walls, which seeks to foster partnerships between churches in Scotland and organisations overseas committed to social and humanitarian transformation. To date partnerships have been established in a plethora of African countries, South Africa and India. A website has been set up to show brief video diaries recorded by the different partner churches telling their stories and witnessing to the benefits of the partnership. This is grass-roots missioning, encouraging local partnership churches to work together to address world development issues. The video clips make use of available technology to highlight the challenges, opportunities, and benefits that result from growing missional communities that have a local and global focus.

The Church of Scotland's transformation in a relatively short time is impressive. Their efforts at re-energising existing congregations and presbyteries to rediscover the radical kingdom ethics at the heart of Jesus' life and teaching have resulted in imaginative and earthed responses. They are reforming modernist and Christendom notions of what it means to be church by shifting the focus to building Christian community where they are, through meeting local needs in practical ways. They are creating networked communities with local and international dimensions that empower Christians to partner each other across geographical and cultural divides. Together these networked partners are tackling the real issues of poverty, environmental destruction and violence. Their approach is holistic, aimed at the whole church, including systems, structures and mindsets. It offers a useful model for Christians struggling with how to respond to the dynamics of change in a postmodern world. Though they do not use descriptive terms like emerging, emergent, or fresh expressions, the above examples are indicators of new or emerging forms of church in contemporary society.

A Challenge for Churches in Ireland

The emerging churches, in the English speaking cultures, have developed out of the broad evangelical movement, which in this postmodern context has been in crisis. Fresh Expressions in England, and Church Without Walls in Scotland, are attempts by mainstream churches to recover the radical ethos and values of Jesus' kingdom vision. The latter, in particular, recognises the need for a whole root and branch transformation, beginning within existing congregations.

Churches in Ireland are also in crisis; having lost their foothold in the public square, they no longer retain the same power base or authoritative role, though some will want to deny this reality. The key issue is how are churches responding? Can they hold together a questioning attitude and openness to God's future, while creatively reconstructing future possibilities that are kingdom-oriented?

Radical transformation is the challenge facing all of the churches in Ireland today. Some are aware of the renewal movements taking place through the emerging church movement, and via links with the Anglican and Methodist Churches in Britain, or through Presbyterian connections with the Church of Scotland.

The recent sexual scandals in the Catholic Church in Ireland raised questions about structures and models of power, shared responsibility, grass roots and central reform. All of the Christian churches in the western world have had a deep problem with the body and physicality, which is a consequence of their patriarchal construction. This includes ambivalent and at times incoherent attitudes and policies in relation to women and sexual orientation. All are challenged, in a postmodernist world, to develop a more holistic anthropology, which will include a more integrated theology of body.

The modernist myth has failed us and needs to be rejected and replaced. Churches in Ireland need to be honest about their negative legacy:

> militarism and [its] ... technology; capitalism and commodification and utilitarianism; colonialism, slavery, the hegemony of the West and the exploitation of the West; the destabilisation of traditional social structures and the rise of individualism[31]

The emerging movements recognise God is calling Christians to remember they are a gathered people on a journey, in exile from the consumerist and militarised mentality that is the paradigm shaping our world. This counter-cultural witness has been crucial to renewal movements within Christianity down through history, and has its source in Jesus the radical Jew who was in the prophetic tradition of Israel.

Personal transformation by itself will not dismantle unjust systems and structures. What is required from Irish churches is a dissociation and rejection of the negative strands of modernity, and

---

31. Grace M. Jantzen, 'On Changing the Imaginary' in *The Blackwell Companion to Postmodern Theology*, ed. Graham Ward, pp. 280–293 (Oxford: Blackwell Publishing, 2001), p. 281.

the adoption of a sociopolitical, economic, and spiritual system that is good news for all of humanity and our planet. For this we need vision, political imagination, and compassionate hearts.

> What would a political order look like were the poetics of the kingdom able to be transformed into political structures? What would it look like if there really were a politics of mercy and compassion, a lifting up of the weakest and most defenceless people at home, a politics of welcoming the stranger and of loving one's enemies abroad? ... A politics not of sovereignty, of top-down power, but a politics that builds from the bottom up ...[32]

In this postmodern culture people within, and outside of, church are searching for meaning, and a spirituality that has an ethical value base and responds to the crises facing local and global communities. There is recognition that in a world where people feel dislocated and isolated the intentional creation of a value-based community is a must.

In Ireland there is need of a reinvigorated spirituality that is committed to embedding justice and striving for peace, where there is an absence of it. This calls for a creative response to global and local inequalities that create divisions, which are unjust and a seedbed of fear, and violence. The consequences of human greed, and the violence of wars, have devastated our environment. We can no longer continue to ignore the signs of ecological breakdown. Churches in Ireland together can find sustainable ways of living, sharing and respecting creation if they accept it as a priority.

A holistic spirituality is informed by a relational understanding of God and faith. Currently the emphasis in Irish churches is on 'faith as assent'; in other words, intellectual assent to a set of propositions, theological formulations, doctrines and right beliefs, i.e. orthodoxy. The emerging church movement is redefining faith as faithfulness; that is faithfulness to our relationship with God.

---

32. John D. Caputo, *What Would Jesus Deconstruct? The Good News of Postmodernism for the Church* (Grand Rapids: Baker Academic, 2007), p. 87.

It is not faithfulness to statements about God, whether biblical, creedal or doctrinal. It means being radically centred in God, loving God and neighbour. The onus is on living faithfully the practice of the ethics of love, justice and peace. This understanding of faith has the potential to transform understandings of church and ways of being church in Ireland.

Brian McLaren, one of the founders and leaders of the emerging movement, names a number of global crises threatening our world that need a response from faith communities; namely, prosperity crises, equity crisis, security crisis and spiritual crisis.[33] He recognises, like Hans Küng before him, that the neighbour religions have a necessary role to play in the healing, or reducing, of these crises. The challenge is for each neighbour religion to find within its faith tradition a framing story capable of giving people alternative direction, vision and values.[34] The framing story for Christians is of course the good news of the kingdom of God.

Neighbour religions also have within their faith traditions a founding story and holistic ethic to enable collaboration on shared values. This ecumenical approach can be played out in local, national, and international arenas. It has the potential to foster relationships across the differences of the neighbour religions, in a way that respects and values the diversity, while finding a core ethical value base that unites participants and enriches praxis. Are Christians in Ireland prepared to take a stand with the 'other' as Jesus did, for the sake of our future and that of generations yet to be born?

---

33. Brian D. McLaren, *Everything Must Change: When the World's Biggest Problems and Jesus' Good News Collide* (Nashville: Thomas Nelson Publishers, 2007), p. 5. The unstable global economy that has ignored environmental limits and economically benefitted a third of the world's population McLaren refers to as the prosperity crisis. The equity crisis is a consequence of the growing gap between the extremely rich and very poor. A militarised world view, ongoing wars throughout the world, and the economic crisis have resulted in a security crisis. Finally, the inability of World Religions to provide an ethical framing story to inspire and direct alternative ways of living and relating has created a spirituality crisis.
34. *Ibid.*, p. 6.

Any change is difficult and risky. The move away from a culture of violence to one of reconciliation was not easy, yet we in Ireland have experienced the benefits to life and community that resulted. Is there a similar commitment to dismantle the theologies and practices that are stifling and redundant in order to recover Jesus' future vision for the earth–human community? Faith is only faith if we are prepared to let go of what we know and wander off traditional routes in response to God's Spirit, which like the Celtic wild goose can never be tamed, fully known, or entirely understood. 'Jesus is not the way unless you are lost, even as Jesus is not the answer unless you have a question.'[35] However, the traveller is not left entirely in the dark.

> We have a sense, a faith, a hope in something, a love of something we know not what, something that calls us on. The great dignity of being human lies in pursuing goals for which there is no guarantee of success and even, at a certain point, no hope of success. But being 'religious people,' by which I mean people who dream of things that have never been and ask 'why not?' we still pursue them.[36]

Unless the churches in Ireland are prepared to shake up the system, and take risks for the sake of God's kingdom, can they be open to the new possibilities and new creation Jesus promised? The courage shown by those in the emerging church movement to question, search, and journey, with one eye on 'the dangerous memories of the suffering Jesus' and another on future possibilities, is a response needed by Irish churches today.[37]

35. Caputo, *What Would Jesus Deconstruct?*, p. 42.
36. *Ibid.*, p. 50.
37. *Ibid.*, p. 61. Caputo is using a phrase coined by John Baptist Metz in *Faith in History and Society*, trans. David Smith (New York: Seabury, 1980), pp. 88–99.

Questions for discussion:
1. What aspects of postmodernism are emerging churches responding to?
2. Are these new models post-evangelical?
3. What insights and practices do these emerging models provide for churches in the Irish context struggling with the challenges of renewal and relevancy?

Conclusion

There are a number of key questions that can helpfully shed light on the nature and presence of church: 'Who constitutes the community of the church? Who speaks in the name of the community? Whose experience is considered revelatory or congruent with earlier privileged revelation? By whom and by what process are these judgements made?'[1]

Hines believes that in order to recover the true nature of church a paradigm shift is needed away from a patriarchal, hierarchical, clerical model of church and toward the creation of a prophetic community characterised by a discipleship of equals.[2] Instead of taking on the role of boundary watcher, she agrees with Schillebeeckx that the church needs to engage with the world, as there is no salvation outside of it.[3]

The focus of this book has been on recovering authentic models of church that might speak to the contemporary Irish context and inspire church communities to risk embracing the exilic paradigm as they search for ways forward. Having reflected on a number of significant biblical, historical and emerging models of church that demonstrate the plurality of approaches to living authentically the Christian witness, I wish to conclude by offering my own vision for church.

My experience within the Irish School of Ecumenics Education for Reconciliation programme has taught me that real change

---

1. Mary Catherine Hilkert, 'Experience And Tradition – Can The Centre Hold? – Revelation' in *Freeing Theology: The Essentials Of Theology In Feminist Perspective*, ed. Catherine Mowry LaCugna, pp. 59–82 (New York: HarperCollins Publishers, 1993), p. 76.
2. Mary E. Hines, 'Community For Liberation – Church' in *Freeing Theology: The Essentials Of Theology In Feminist Perspective*, ed. Catherine Mowry LaCugna, pp. 161–184 (New York: HarperCollins Publishers, 1993), pp. 163–164.
3. *Ibid.*, p. 164.

occurs in grass-roots communities, and that education for change is a necessary part of any transformative process. A privatistic, individualist model of faith has failed the people of Ireland; it has fostered religious sectarianism and remained silent in the face of injustice, violence and hatred. My vision for church in Ireland will find expression in the creation of grass-roots, localised, ecumenical communities that honour the gospel vision of a discipleship of equals. A primary concern guiding these communities will be the living out of the kingdom of God values in a spirit of compassionate caring, justice, truthfulness and peace. The defining characteristics of these ecumenical communities will be: openness, transparency, respect for all, concern to promote women's active involvement and leadership, engagement with the ecological crisis that takes seriously environmental concerns locally and globally, commitment to dialogue and learning, and ongoing reflection on reconciliation praxis. These communities will be places where people can gather to share their experiences, heal their hurts and repair their relationships. Leadership in these communities will be shared and members will be encouraged to use their gifts in the living out of God's kingdom ethics.

Liturgies of reconciliation and healing with peoples and the earth will be developed within the communities that will connect with the Irish context, as well as issues of reconciliation on the world stage. All will be welcome to these liturgies and, when it is appropriate, they can be celebrated in other significant places in the wider community, where the power of God's Spirit is needed to bring healing and reconciliation.

The communities will also be places where spiritualities of reconciliation can develop. Spiritualities that are rooted in a vision of God in solidarity with all of creation; a God whom men and women can equally identify with, who is praised using a plethora of metaphors; a God who is prepared to take risks for the sake of reconciliation and is concerned to ensure that the poor, marginalised and strangers are treated with generosity and justice. Also spiritualities in touch with the Wisdom/*Sophia* tradition that recognises Christ in all places and peoples, furthering God's reign of justice, righteousness, compassion and peace.

As in the early Christian communities, church or *ekklesia* will be defined by the nature of these ecumenical communities. They will be alternative church to the patriarchal, dualistic model of church currently prevalent. And as these ecumenical communities take root new questions will emerge that will assist ongoing reflection and development.

Readers will have their own visions for church and the sharing of these will, I believe, contribute to the growing of authentic faith communities. My hope is that, whatever forms they take, the distinguishing characteristic of each will be a commitment to living out the counter-cultural ethics of God's Kingdom.

Bibliography

Anderson, Paul N., 'Jesus and Peace' in *The Church's Peace Witness*, eds Marlin E. Miller and Barbara Nelson Gingerich, pp. 104–130 (Michigan: William B. Eerdmans Publishing Company, 1994).

Armstrong, Karen, *A Short History of Myth* (Edinburgh: Canongate Books Ltd, 2005).

Barrett, Lois Y., 'The Fragmentation of the Church and Its Unity in Peacemaking: A Mennonite Perspective' in *The Fragmentation of the Church and Its Unity in Peacemaking*, eds Jeffrey Gros and John D. Rempel, pp. 103–118 (Cambridge: William B. Eerdmans Publishing Company, 2001).

Berquist, Jon L., *Judaism in Persia's Shadow: A Social and Holistic Approach* (Minneapolis: Fortress Press, 1995).

Berresford Ellis, Peter, *Celtic Women: Women in Celtic Society and Literature* (London: Constable and Company Ltd, 1995).

Bitel, Lisa M., '"Hail Brigit!" Gender, Authority and Worship in Early Ireland' in *Irish Women's History*, eds Alan Hayes and Diane Urquhart, pp. 1–14 (Dublin: Irish Academic Press, 2004).

— *Isle of the Saints: Monastic Settlement and Christian Community in Early Ireland* (Cork: Cork University Press, 1990).

— *Land of Women: Tales of Sex and Gender from Early Ireland* (London: Cornell University Press, 1996).

Blough, Neal, 'Globalization and Claiming Truth' in *Seeking Cultures of Peace: A Peace Church Conversation*, eds Fernando Enns, Scott Holland and Ann K. Riggs, pp. 45–61 (Telford PA: Cascadia Publishing House, 2004).

Borg, Marcus J. and John Dominic Crossan, *The First Paul: Reclaiming the radical visionary behind the church's conservative icon* (London: SPCK, 2009).

Bradley, Ian, *Colonies of Heaven: Celtic Models for Today's Church* (London: Darton, Longman and Todd, 2000).

Brueggemann, Walter, *An Introduction to the Old Testament: The Canon and Christian Imagination* (London: Westminster John Knox Press, 2003).

— *Cadences of Home: Preaching among Exiles* (Louisville: Westminster John Knox Press, 1997).

— *Theology of the Old Testament: Testimony, Dispute, Advocacy* (Minneapolis: Fortress Press, 1997).

— *The Word Militant: Preaching a Decentering Word* (Minneapolis: Fortress Press, 2007).

Callen, Barry L., *Radical Christianity: The Believers Church Tradition in Christianity's History and Future* (Indiana: Evangel Publishing House, 1999).

Caputo, John D., *What Would Jesus Deconstruct? The Good News of Postmodernism for the Church* (Grand Rapids: Baker Academic, 2007).

Carter, Warren, *Matthew and the Margins: A Sociopolitical and Religious Reading* (Maryknoll, NY: Orbis Books, 2000).

Chung, Sook-Ja, 'Women Church in Korea: Voices and Visions', *The Ecumenical Review*, 53/1 (January 2001): pp. 72–81.

Church of England Report, *Mission-Shaped Church: Church planting and fresh expressions of church in a changing context* (London: Church House Publishing, 2004).

Cogitosus, 'Life of St Brigid the Virgin' in *St Patrick's World: The Christian Culture Of Ireland's Apostolic Age*, ed. Liam De Paor, pp. 207–224 (Dublin: Four Courts Press, 1996).

Concannon, Maureen, *The Sacred Whore: Sheela Goddess of the Celts* (Cork: The Collins Press, 2004).

Condren, Mary, *The Serpent and the Goddess: Women, Religion, and Power in Celtic Ireland* (San Francisco: Harper and Row, 1989).

Crosby, Michael H., 'Matthew's Gospel: The Disciples' Call to Justice' in *The New Testament: Introducing the Way of Discipleship*, eds Wess Howard-Brook and Sharon H. Ringe, pp. 16–39 (New York: Orbis Books, 2002).

Daly, Gabriel, *One Church: Two Indispensable Values – Protestant Principle and Catholic Substance*, Occasional Paper 4 (Dublin: Irish School of Ecumenics, 1998).

Davies, Oliver, *Celtic Spirituality* (New Jersey: Paulist Press, 1999).

De Paor, Liam, *St Patrick's World: The Christian Culture of Ireland's Apostolic Age* (Dublin: Four Courts Press Ltd, 1993).

Deats, Richard, 'The Global Spread of Active Nonviolence' in *Peace Is The Way: Writings on Nonviolence from the Fellowship of Reconciliation*, ed. Walter Wink, pp. 283–295 (New York: Orbis Books, 2003).

Doherty, Jerry C., *A Celtic Model of Ministry: The Reawakening of Community Spirituality* (Minnesota: The Liturgical Press, 2003).

Donfried, Karl P., 'The Imperial Cults of Thessalonica and Political Conflict in 1 Thessalonians' in *Paul and Empire: Religion and Power in Roman Imperial Society*, ed. Richard A. Horsley, pp. 215–223 (Pennsylvania: Trinity Press International, 1997).

Douglas Hall, John, *The End of Christendom and the Future of Christianity* (Pennsylvania: Trinity Press International, 1997).

— *Thinking the Faith: Christian Theology in a North American Context* (Minneapolis: Fortress Press, 1991).

Dungan, David R., *Constantine's Bible: Politics and the Making of the New Testament* (London: SCM Press, 2006).

Elliott, Marianne, *When God Took Sides: Religion and Identity in Ireland: Unfinished History* (Oxford: Oxford University Press, 2009).

Estep, William R., *The Anabaptist Story: An Introduction to Sixteenth-Century Anabaptism* (3rd edn, Cambridge: William B. Eerdmans Publishing Company, 1996).

Farley, Edward, *Deep Symbols: Their Postmodern Effacement and Reclamation* (Harrisburg, PA: Trinity International Press, 1996).

Freyne, Seán, *Jesus, A Jewish Galilean: A new reading of the Jesus-story* (London: T & T Clark International, Imprint of Continuum International Publishing Group, 2004).

Fuellenbach, John, *The Kingdom of God: The Message of Jesus Today* (New York: Orbis Books, 1995).

Gaudium et Spes in *Documents of Vatican II: Conciliar and Post Conciliar Documents*, ed. Austin Flannery, pp. 903–1001 (Dublin: Dominican Publications, 1975).

Gibbs, Eddie and Ryan K. Bolger, *Emerging Churches: Creating Christian Community in Postmodern Cultures* (London: SPCK, 2006).

Gritsch, Eric W., *Toxic Spirituality: Four Enduring Temptations of Christian Faith* (Minneapolis: Fortress Press, 2009).

Hanson, Paul D., *The People Called: The Growth of Community in the Bible* (San Francisco: Harper & Row, 1987).

Harrington, Christina, *Women In A Celtic Church: Ireland 450–1150* (Oxford: Oxford University Press, 2002).

Hilkert, Mary Catherine, 'Experience And Tradition – Can The Centre Hold? – Revelation' in *Freeing Theology: The Essentials Of Theology In Feminist Perspective*, ed. Catherine Mowry LaCugna, pp. 59–82 (New York: HarperCollins Publishers, 1993).

Hines, Mary E., 'Community For Liberation – Church' in *Freeing Theology: The Essentials of Theology in Feminist Perspective*, ed. Catherine Mowry LaCugna, pp. 161–184 (New York: HarperCollins Publishers, 1993).

Hodgson, Peter C., *Winds of the Spirit: A Constructive Christian Theology* (Louisville: Westminster John Knox Press, 1994).

Horsley, Richard A., 'Building An Alternative Society: An Intro-duction' in *Paul and Empire: Religion and Power in Roman Imperial Society*, ed. Richard A Horsley, pp. 206–214 (Pennsylvania: Trinity Press International, 1997).

— '1 Corinthians: A Case Study of Paul's Assembly as an Alternative Society' in *Paul and Empire: Religion and Power in Roman Imperial Society*, ed. Richard A. Horsley, pp. 242–252 (Pennsylvania: Trinity Press International, 1997).

Jantzen, Grace M. 'On Changing the Imaginary' in *The Blackwell Companion to Postmodern Theology*, ed. Graham Ward, pp. 280–293 (Oxford: Blackwell Publishing, 2001).

— 'The Courtroom and the Garden: Gender and Violence in Christendom' in *Violence Against Women in Contemporary World Religion: Roots and Cures*, eds Daniel C. Maguire and Sa'diyya Shaikh, pp. 29–48 (Cleveland: Pilgrim Press, 2007).

Johnson, Elizabeth A., *She Who Is: The Mystery of God in Feminist Theological Discourse* (New York: The Crossroad Publishing Company, 1995).

— 'Imaging God, Embodying Christ: Women as a Sign of the Times' in *The Church Women Want*, ed. Elizabeth A. Johnston, pp. 44–59 (New York: The Crossroad Publishing Company, 2002).

King, Karen L., 'Canonization and Marginalization: Mary of Magdala' in 'Women's Sacred Scriptures', *Concilium* 1998/3, eds Kwok Pui-Lan and Elisabeth Schussler Fiorenza, pp. 29–36. (London: SCM Press, 1998).

Kreider, Alan, *The Change of Conversion and the Origin of Christendom* (Harrisburg: Trinity Press International, 1999).

Kung, Hans, *Women in Christianity* (London: Continuum, 2001).

Lawlor, Pearse, *The Burnings 1920* (Cork: Mercier Press, 2009).

Liechty, Joseph and Cecelia Clegg, *Moving Beyond Sectarianism: Religion, Conflict, and Reconciliation in Northern Ireland* (Dublin: The Columba Press, 2001).

Long, Jimmy, *Emerging Hope: A Strategy for Reaching Postmodern Generations* (Illinois: InterVarsity Press, 2004).

McCartney, Clem, 'Conclusions – The Social Witness of a Peculiar People' in *Coming From The Silence: Quaker Peacebuilding Initiative in Northern Ireland 1969–2007*, eds Ann Le Mare and Felicity McCartney, pp. 163–171 (York: William Sessions Ltd, 2009).

McCartney, Felicity, 'Looking Behind Quaker Work' in *Coming From The Silence: Quaker Peacebuilding Initiative in Northern Ireland 1969–2007*, eds Ann Le Mare and Felicity McCartney, pp. 1–15 (York: William Sessions Ltd, 2009).

MacCulloch, Diarmaid, *A History of Christianity: The First Three Thousand Years* (London: Allen Lane, Imprint of Penguin Books, 2009).

McDonagh, Enda, *Between Chaos and New Creation* (Dublin: Gill & Macmillan, 1986).

McLaren, Brian D., *Everything Must Change: When the World's Biggest Problems and Jesus' Good News Collide* (Nashville: Thomas Nelson Publishers, 2007).

MacLeod, John, *Highlanders: A History of the Gaels* (London: Hodder and Stoughton, 1996).

Maguire, William A., *Belfast: A History* (Lancaster: Carnegie Publishing Ltd, 2009).

Malone, Mary T., *Women and Christianity, Volume 3: From the Reformation to the 21st Century* (Dublin: The Columba Press, 2003).

Miller, Marlin E., 'Toward Acknowledging Together the Apostolic Character of the Church's Peace Witness' in *The Church's Peace Witness*, eds Marlin E. Miller and Barbara Nelson Gingerich, pp. 196–207 (Michigan: William B. Eerdmans Publishing Company, 1994).

Minear, Paul S., *Images of the Church in the New Testament* (Cambridge: James Clarke & Co., 1960, repr. 2007).

Murphy, Claire C., *Woman as Church: The challenge to change* (Dublin: Gill & Macmillan Ltd, 1997).

Murray, Stuart, *Church After Christendom* (London: Paternoster Press, 2004).

Nelson-Pallmeyer, Jack, *Jesus Against Christianity* (Harrisburg, Pennsylvania: Trinity Press International, 2001).

Noll, K. L., *Canaan and Israel in Antiquity: An Introduction* (London: Sheffield Academic Press, Imprint of Continuum International Publishing Group, 2001).

Ó Cróinín, Dáibhí, *Early Medieval Ireland 400–1200* (London: Longman Group Ltd, 1995).

Osiek, Carolyn and Margaret Y. Macdonald with Janet H. Tulloch, *A Woman's Place: House Churches in Earliest Christianity* (Minneapolis: Fortress Press, 2006).

Osiek, Carolyn, 'Reading the Bible as Women' in *The New Interpreter's Bible: A Commentary in 12 Volumes, Volume 1*, ed. Leander E. Keck, pp. 181–187 (Edinburgh: Abingdon Press, 1994).

Paxson Jr., Thomas D., 'The Peace Testimony of the Religious Society of Friends' in *The Fragmentation of the Church and Its Unity in Peacemaking*, eds Jeffrey Gros and John D. Rempel, pp. 103–118 (Cambridge: William B. Eerdmans Publishing Company, 2001).

Quaker Faith & Practice, *The book of Christian discipline of the Yearly Meeting of the Religious Society of Friends (Quakers) in Britain* (3rd edn, London: The Yearly Meeting of the Religious Society of Friends (Quakers) in Britain, 2005).

Radford Ruether, Rosemary, *Sexism And God-Talk: Towards A Feminist Theology* (Boston: Beacon Press, 1983).

— *Women-Church: Theology & Practice of Feminist Liturgical Communities* (San Francisco: Harper & Row, 1986).

Richter, Michael, *Medieval Ireland: The Enduring Tradition* (Dublin: Gill & Macmillan Ltd, 1988).

Rollins, Peter, *How (Not) To Speak Of God* (London: SPCK, 2006).

— *The Fidelity of Betrayal: Towards A Church Beyond Belief* (London: SPCK, 2008).

Russell, Letty, *Church in the Round: Feminist Interpretation of the Church* (Louisville: Westminster John Knox Press, 1993).

Schneiders, Sandra M., *Beyond Patching: Faith And Feminism In The Catholic Church* (New Jersey: Paulist Press International, 1991).

Schussler Fiorenza, Elisabeth, *In Memory Of Her: A Feminist Theological Reconstruction Of Christian Origins* (London: SCM Press Ltd, 1983).

— 'The Praxis of Coequal Discipleship' in *Paul and Empire: Religion and Power in Roman Imperial Society,* ed. Richard A. Horsley, pp. 224–241 (Pennsylvania: Trinity Press International, 1997).

Smith, Abraham, 'Unmasking the Powers: Towards a Postcolonial Analysis of 1 Thessalonians' in *Paul and the Roman Imperial Order*, ed. Richard A. Horsley, pp. 47–66 (London: Trinity Press International, 2004).

Smith, David, *Mission After Christendom* (London: Darton, Longman and Todd Ltd, 2003).

Staunton, Michael, *The Illustrated Story of Christian Ireland From St Patrick to the Peace Process* (Dublin: Emerald Press, 2001).

Stassen, Glen H. and David P. Gushee, *Kingdom Ethics: Following Jesus in Contemporary Context* (Downers Grove, Illinois: InterVarsity Press, 2003).

Swindler, Leonard, *Jesus was a Feminist: What the Gospels Reveal about His Revolutionary Perspective* (Plymouth: Sheed & Ward, 2007).

Thom, Catherine, *Early Irish Monasticism: An Understanding of its Cultural Roots* (London: T & T Clarke, 2006).

Tickle, Phyllis, *The Great Emergence: How Christianity is Changing and Why* (Grand Rapids: Baker Books, 2008).

Tomlinson, Dave, *The Post-Evangelical* (London: SPCK, 1995).

Watson, Natalie K., *Introducing Feminist Ecclesiology* (London: Sheffield Academic Press, Imprint of Continuum International Publishing Group, 2002).

Weaver, J. Denny, 'Violence in Christian Theology' in *Teaching Peace: Nonviolence and the Liberal Arts*, eds J. Denny Weaver and Gerald Biesecker-Mast, pp. 39–52 (Oxford: Rowman & Littlefield Publishers Inc., 2003).

Wilson-Hartgrove, Jonathan, *New Monasticism: What It Has To Say To Today's Church* (Grand Rapids: Brazos Press, 2008).

Yee, Gale A., *Poor Banished Children of Eve: Woman as Evil in the Hebrew Bible* (Minneapolis: Fortress Press, 2003).

Yoder, John Howard, *The Royal Priesthood: Essays Ecclesiological and Ecumenical* (Grand Rapids: Eerdmans, 1994).

Websites

'About', *Ikon* [website] <http://www.peterrollins.net/about.html> accessed 21 July 2010.

Church Without Walls report, *The Church of Scotland* [website], <http://www.churchofscotland.org.uk/churchwithout-walls/index.htm> accessed 24 July 2010.

The Church of England [website] <http://www.cofe.anglican.org/-info/yearreview/dec05/freshexpressions.html> accessed 24 July 2010

Mobsby, Ian, 'The Emerging Church in the UK: Personal Reflections', *Emerging Church* [website] <http://www.emergingchurch.info/reflection/ianmobsby2/index.htm> accessed 23 July 2010.

'What is a fresh expression?', *Fresh Expressions* [website] http://www.freshexpressions.org.uk/about/whatis